SIXTH EDITION

Idaho

SUPPLEMENT FOR

Modern Real Estate Practice

R. GAIL HEIST
W. MIKE LOEGERING
CONSULTING EDITORS

Real Estate Education Company
a division of Dearborn Financial Publishing, Inc.

While a great deal of care has been taken to provide accurate and current information, the ideas, suggestions, general principles and conclusions presented in this text are subject to local, state and federal laws and regulations, court cases and any revisions of same. The reader is thus urged to consult legal counsel regarding any points of law—this publication should not be used as a substitute for competent legal advice.

Acquisitions Editor: Margaret M. Maloney
Associate Development Editor: Laurie A. Connole
Project Editor: Vickie Woodruff
Cover Design: Jim Buddenbaum

Published by Real Estate Education Company,
a division of Dearborn Financial Publishing, Inc.

Printed in the United States of America.

91 92 93 10 9 8 7 6 5 4 3 2

Library of Congress Cataloging-in-Publication Data

Idaho supplement for Modern real estate practice.—6th ed. / R. Gail
   Heist, W. Mike Loegering, consulting editors.
         p. cm.
      "In cooperation with the Idaho Real Estate Commission."
      Includes index.
      ISBN 0-79310-052-6
         1. Real estate business—Law and legislation—Idaho. 2. Vendors
and purchasers—Idaho. 3. Real property—Idaho. 4. Real estate
business—Idaho. I. Heist, R. Gail. II. Loegering, W. Mike.
III. Galaty, Fillmore W. Modern real estate practice. IV. Real
Estate Education Company. V. Idaho Real Estate Commission.
KF2042.R4G34   1990 Suppl.2
346.79604'37—dc20   90-49200
[347.9606437]   CIP

Table of Contents

Preface

Real estate practice in any state is based on the state's constitution, laws, regulations and court decisions in addition to fundamental federal laws and regulations. Each state's legislature, courts and commissions make laws and regulations governing activities in that state.

The Idaho legislature convenes each year on the second Monday in January. It also may be called into special session by order of the governor. In any of these sessions, new laws may be passed or changes made in existing laws that affect real estate practice.

Also, the practice of real estate in any specific location in Idaho may be influenced by local agencies, bureaus and organizations, such as county and city governments or local boards of REALTORS®, and by the controls and/or customs initiated by these organizations.

The purpose of this real estate Supplement is to discuss the body of laws and operating procedures applicable to the state of Idaho. This Supplement builds on basic information presented in the text, *Modern Real Estate Practice*, 12th edition, by Galaty, Allaway and Kyle, also published by Real Estate Education Company, Chicago. Although every effort has been made not to duplicate basic information covered in the text, the student should be careful to adapt the information in *Modern Real Estate Practice* to the special state-specific facts covered in this Supplement. Therefore, first study the text lesson and then refer to the same subject area in this Supplement.

The Supplement is closely keyed to the basic text to facilitate easy reference from one to the other. Each chapter number corresponds to that chapter in *Modern Real Estate Practice*. Some chapters in the basic text have no related lessons in the Supplement because the subject matter does not involve laws or practices that vary significantly from state to state.

Following each chapter are questions drawn from material in the text and in the Supplement. These tests can be both evaluative and educational. Be certain that you understand and are able to answer each question before you go on to the next chapter. An Answer Key for all of the tests is included at the back of this Supplement.

Throughout your real estate course, you will be studying and taking tests in preparation for the Idaho Real Estate License Examination. All applicants for real estate licensing in Idaho must pass a standardized examination. In an additional section of the Idaho exam, the questions pertain to Idaho laws and regulations. The *Idaho Supplement for Modern Real Estate Practice*, 6th edition, includes specific Idaho legislation as well as general information you will need to know in order to pass the examination.

CONSULTING EDITORS

R. Gail Heist, GRI, is the director of Pioneer Real Estate School in Boise, Idaho. He is also broker-owner of Professional Real Estate Services in Boise, Idaho. Mr. Heist received a bachelor of science in marketing from the University of Utah and a master of business administration from Boise State University. He spent 12 years as a full-time faculty member in the School of Business at Boise State University, where he helped develop the baccalaureate degree program in real estate. He has been actively involved in real estate as a developer, consultant and broker for more than 25 years and is certified by the Idaho Real Estate Commission to teach the following courses: Essentials of Real Estate Practices, Real Estate Practices, Brokerage Administration, Real Estate Valuation and Analysis, Continuing Education II. For several years Mr. Heist has been an instructor for the Idaho Association of REALTORS® in the Graduate REALTORS® Institute Program, teaching topics such as Pricing the Property, Common Forms of Ownership, Resort Time-Shares, Industrial Real Estate, Real Estate Development, Closing the Transaction and Property Management.

W. Mike Loegering, GRI, received his bachelor of science in business administration from Woodbury College in Los Angeles, California. He has been an Idaho real estate instructor for over 16 years, two of which he served as a full-time real estate instructor at Boise State University, where he taught Fundamentals of Real Estate, Fundamentals of Real Estate Appraisal, Real Estate Finance, Real Estate Brokerage Administration. He also helped to establish a real estate advisory council for the College of Business, and served for four years as a member of the adjunct real estate faculty. Mr. Loegering currently holds an active associate broker's license, is a "fee" review appraiser for HUD and is an independent real estate instructor certified by the Idaho Real Estate Commission to teach Essentials of Real Estate, Real Estate Practices and Continuing Education Course II. He has taught sales and broker license preparatory courses for the Idaho Real Estate Commission, owned and operated his own certified real estate proprietary school and was appointed to a four-year term on the Idaho Real Estate Education Council, which is responsible for promoting high quality real estate education throughout the state. Mr. Loegering has been involved in the real estate industry for over 29 years, a career that has included the title insurance business, lending, residential appraising, and real estate brokerage. More than 20 of those years have been spent in Idaho as a licensed sales associate, associate broker/branch manager, owner-broker and franchisee of a real estate company and an associate broker/consultant.

Thanks are extended to the following members of the Idaho Real Estate Education Council for their reviews of the manuscript: Freeman Duncan, Joan Brawley, Marvis Brice, Nila Briggs, Maurice Clifton and Jeri Pyeatt.

Credit for permission to use forms is given by the Boise Board of REALTORS® and the Pioneer Title Company of Canyon County.

4

Real Estate Brokerage

In Idaho a person must be a licensed real estate broker to perform, negotiate or attempt to perform or negotiate for others for a fee any of the following activities involving real property or business opportunities: listing, selling, buying, exchanging, procuring prospects, closing transactions or otherwise dealing in options. In other words a person must have a broker's license to operate a brokerage and collect commissions. *See* Chapter 13 of this Supplement for a list of situations for which a broker's license is not needed (Section 54-2024).

REAL ESTATE LICENSE LAW

Idaho real estate licenses are granted by the *Idaho Real Estate Commission* under the provisions of the *Idaho Real Estate License Law*. This law and the Commission's *Rules and Regulations* regulate and place restrictions on the activities of brokers and salespeople. Many of the provisions were created to implement and enforce the law of agency in broker-client relationships. The specific provisions of this law will be discussed in Chapter 13 of this Supplement.

The status of Idaho's entire real estate industry has been elevated since the Real Estate License Law was first enacted in 1947. The law was initiated by the industry and is enforced by the industry at the licensee's expense. It places restrictions on the actions of people in the real estate business to protect the public they serve. In addition the law requires licensed real estate salespersons to further their education if they wish to become brokers. The Idaho Real Estate Commission also encourages all real estate licensees to increase their education and knowledge to better serve their customers and clients. As a result of the improved services offered, the public has come to recognize the real estate broker or salesperson as a professional—a specialist in real estate.

THE BROKERAGE BUSINESS

Agency

In Idaho a real estate broker is legally an agent. An associate broker or salesperson is an agent of the broker and a subagent of the principal. An agent or subagent is classified as either a general agent or a special agent, based on the extent of his or her authority. A *general agent* is authorized to represent the principal in *all matters or in all matters concerning one area of the principal's interest*, such as the principal's business affairs. A *special agent* is authorized to represent the principal in *one specific transaction or piece of business* and with *limited* authority to act. Therefore the real estate broker is a special agent. For example, the act of listing real estate for sale creates a special agency because the principal retains full authority to accept or reject offers and to sign documents.

When a real estate licensee accepts the responsibility from a principal to accept or reject the terms and conditions contained in purchase agreements or to sign warranty deeds, mortgages or other documents for the principal, the real estate agent becomes a general agent and must recognize the increased responsibilities and liabilities that result from being a general agent.

The agency relationship is created when a real estate licensee is engaged by a client and authorized, either verbally or in writing, to transact business on the client's behalf. When representing their principals, brokers and salespeople must comply with the fiduciary obligations created by the law of agency. The broker's fiduciary obligations under the law of agency are described in Chapter 5 of the text.

Effective January 1, 1989, Idaho joined several other states mandating agency disclosure by requiring all licensees to make prompt disclosure of their agency relationships to all prospective buyers and sellers. The disclosure must occur prior to the establishment of an agency relationship; and at the time a real estate purchase and sale agreement is signed by a buyer and a seller, each will be asked to confirm:

1.   that they received the brochure prepared by the Idaho Real Estate Commission,

2.   who if anyone represented them in the transaction, and

3.   that they read and understood the contents of the brochure.

The fact that a licensee disclosed his or her agency relationship with a buyer and seller does not mean that the licensee could not have created an inadvertent dual agency. For example, if you are working with a buyer you previously represented as a seller, are representing a relative or a close personal friend, or have become involved in an exchange, it would be wise to confer with your broker or get a legal opinion before an undisclosed dual agency is created.

Ethical and legal considerations. Although the broker is usually the agent of the seller in a real estate sales transaction, a prospective buyer sometimes may retain a broker to look for a parcel of real estate that meets specific requirements. A broker may not represent both parties to a transaction without disclosing his or her dual agency to both principals and receiving their informed consent. Whether the broker can receive a commission from both parties is a matter requiring mutual agreement of the parties. The client relationship always should be fully defined and disclosed.

The law of agency clearly states that an agent or subagent owes the highest fiduciary duty to his or her principal and must act solely in the principal's best interests. This does not, however, relieve the licensee of responsibility treating the other party to a transaction fairly. Moreover, a licensee shall not discourage either party from consulting an attorney regarding the transaction.

Listing agreement. A document that creates an agency between broker and seller is a listing agreement. This document has two parts: (1) a contract between broker and seller stating the amount of commission the broker will earn as well as all other terms of the agreement including the granting of the agency relationship by the listing seller to the real estate broker, and (2) data about the real estate being offered for sale. *A listing contract must be in writing and signed by all owners of the property and the broker* before the broker is entitled to collect a commission for doing what he or she was hired to do. Suppose, for example, a property owner asks a broker to sell some property and promises to pay the broker a commission, and the broker agrees and sells the property. Suppose further that the owner, who obviously has benefited from the broker's services, then refuses to pay. The broker can take legal action to make the owner pay only if he or she has a written listing contract. A signed written agreement provides proof of what both parties promised to do.

The Broker's Commission

The broker's commission, usually a specified percentage of the final sales price, is stated as one of the terms of the listing agreement. The amount or exact percentage the broker will receive is a matter to be decided by the broker and the principal in each transaction. Idaho law and the Rules and Regulations of the Idaho Real Estate Commission do not set uniform commission rates or approve of agreements to standardize rates. Any agreement among brokers to set a fixed commission rate is considered *price fixing* and a violation of the Sherman Antitrust Act. All real estate commissions are strictly and fully negotiable between the principal/payer and the broker.

Broker's Liability

A tort is a private or civil wrong or injury committed upon a person or a person's property not arising from a breach of contract. Negligence is a tort; so is fraud. As an agent a real estate broker is liable (legally responsible) to his or her principal for torts as well as for breach of contract. Brokers also may be liable for acts of the salespeople who represent them. In addition salespeople may be held personally liable for their own torts. Where third parties (such as purchasers or prospective purchasers) are concerned, brokers are always liable for their own torts. The principal, at whose direction the broker acts, may or may not be liable for the broker's torts, depending on the situation.

As discussed in the text, brokers make many statements or representations regarding the condition of the property being offered for sale during the course of a real estate transaction. Certain types of statements made by the broker that are in fact false are not considered torts. Statements openly made as opinions or predictions, statements or promises that become part of the contract and honest mistakes fall into this category. The broker can, however, be held liable for false statements made or represented to be fact.

The three types of misrepresentation are *innocent*, *negligent* and *fraudulent*. An *innocent* misrepresentation is an inadvertent misstatement of a material fact or a false statement that the speaker does not know is false. A statement made by a broker based on false information supplied by the principal is included in this category because the deliberate misrepresentation was made by the principal, not by the broker. However, brokers and salespersons are held to a certain level of expertise as professionals and they should know that any material statement should be verified. *Example:* During the middle of winter the listing broker asks the seller if the central air-conditioning works. The broker is told that it does work. The listing broker then tells a prospective buyer that the air-conditioning works "just fine," and relying on that information, the buyer purchases the property. In the summer the air conditioner does not work. A contract may be canceled on the basis of a broker's innocent misrepresentation.

A *negligent* misrepresentation is a misstatement of a material fact or a false statement that the speaker believes to be true but does not have reasonable proof of its accuracy. Such statements are irresponsibly made, and a broker can be held liable for making them. *Example:* The listing broker asks the owner what the zoning is on the property, and the owner says "I think it is zoned multifamily." The listing broker then enters multifamily zoning on the listing agreement. The broker has a responsibility to verify the seller's statements before representing them to a prospective buyer.

A *fraudulent* misrepresentation is a false statement regarding a material fact that is made by a person who knows the statement is false. *Example:* The listing broker is told by the owner that the roof leaks when a moderately strong north wind accompanies a rainstorm. The listing broker elects not to disclose this fact to a prospective purchaser because the wind seldom blows from the north during a rainstorm. Deliberately or willfully *concealing* a material fact from a prospective purchaser also falls under this area of misrepresentation.

Fraud

Fraud is defined as:

1. a deceitful practice or material misstatement of a material fact,

2. known to be false,

3. done with intent to deceive or with reckless indifference as to its truth, and

4. relied on by the injured party to his or her damage.

Fraudulent acts may be actual or constructive. *Actual* fraud involves acts or omissions deliberately intended to deceive or to induce another to enter into a contract. *Example:* A selling broker produces an altered appraisal report on a particular property purporting the value of the property to be several thousand dollars higher than its true value. Based on the representations made, a buyer purchases the property.

Constructive fraud refers to acts or omissions not intended to be fraudulent but in effect create a fraudulent situation. *Example:* An owner of real estate gift deeds property to a "friend" for love and affection. Later, creditors who have a valid claim against the former owner find out about this transfer and have it "set aside" as an act of fraud. (There may not have been any *intent* to defraud the creditors, but in fact constructive fraud or fraud in law exists.) Note that constructive fraud often consists of a breach of duty arising out of the fiduciary relationship.

The key factor in defining a case of fraud rests on the importance of the information being misrepresented and whether the other party has a right to rely on that information to make a decision and/or enter into a contract. In most real estate transactions both seller and buyer have the right to assume a broker's statements are true.

A person found guilty of fraud may be subject to criminal as well as civil penalties.

Agreement Between Broker and Salesperson

The broker is advised to have a written agreement with each salesperson. The actual form of contract between a broker and a salesperson depends on whether the salesperson is to operate as the broker's employee or as an independent contractor (the distinction between the two is discussed in the main text). Throughout Idaho, most brokers engage salespeople as independent contractors. To qualify as an independent contractor for federal tax purposes, as outlined in Section 3508 of the Internal Revenue Code (effective 1983), a real estate salesperson must meet three conditions:

1. The salesperson must be a licensed real estate agent.

2. Substantially all of the salesperson's compensation for services as a real estate agent must be directly related to sales or other performance output, rather than to hours worked.

3. Services must be performed pursuant to a written contract that provides that the individual will not be treated as an employee for federal tax purposes.

The independent contractor arrangement does not protect the broker from tort and contract liability owing to the salesperson's actions. Any contract creating a broker-independent contractor relationship should include the following provisions:

1. The broker agrees to make current listings available to the salesperson and to provide advice, instruction and full cooperation. Furthermore the salesperson may share the broker's office facilities.

2. The salesperson agrees to work diligently to sell property listed with the broker and to solicit additional listings for the broker. The salesperson also agrees to conduct business and regulate his or her habits to enhance the broker's goodwill and reputation; to comply with all laws, rules and regulations, and codes of ethics that apply to real estate salespeople; and to conduct himself or herself in service to the public so that both broker and salesperson receive the greatest possible profit.

3. The contract specifies the exact amount of compensation to be paid the salesperson for both sales and listing commissions and describes how listing commissions will be paid. The contract also provides that the salesperson's commission will not be due and payable until it is received in cash or other acceptable preagreed-on form by the broker. There should be a provision authorizing the broker to deduct from the subagent's share of the commission any expenses incurred in collecting commissions, such as attorney's fees or court costs. The contract should stipulate how a dispute between two salespeople in the office over the division of a commission will be settled. This may be handled in one of two ways: The contract could state that such a decision will be made by the supervising broker or (perhaps more fairly) the contract could provide that such disputes be submitted to arbitration.

4. The contract defines the relationship between the broker and the salesperson, who is a subagent only with respect to customers or clients for whom services are performed. In his or her relationship with the broker, the salesperson is an independent contractor and not a servant, employee, joint venturer or partner of the broker.

5. The broker is authorized, when necessary, to take notes or security payment of commissions. In such instances the salesperson's share of the commission will be paid proportionately as the commission is received by the broker.

6. The broker is authorized to make settlements of commission claims when he or she feels uncertain about the outcome of a legal suit to recover the commission and chooses a settlement as the best course of action. This clause also authorizes the broker to make a settlement with a purchaser who has forfeited earnest money.

7. The contract provides for a situation in which the purchaser's earnest money is forfeited and no settlement has been made. In this situation a broker safely cannot pay the salesperson's share of the commission out of the forfeited money because the possibility exists that the purchaser might later bring successful legal action against the broker for the return of the earnest money.

8. The salesperson agrees to furnish his or her own automotive transportation and to carry liability insurance, which protects the broker in the event the salesperson has an automobile accident in the course of his or her work for the broker.

9. Either party may terminate the relationship upon giving written notice to the other. However, some contracts specify that written notice must be given a certain number of days in advance. (The Idaho Real Estate License Law requires certain formalities when a real estate

salesperson changes employment. It is recommended, but not necessary, that these also be incorporated into the contract.)

10. After the contract is terminated the salesperson must not use to his or her advantage, or to the advantage of any other person or corporation, any information gained from the broker's files or business. In addition the salesperson must return all stationery, legal papers and any other of the broker's property. The contract also may provide for payment of commissions earned but not yet paid and for a future right to commissions on existing active listings that are sold after the salesperson's voluntary or involuntary termination.

In addition to these provisions, contracts often provide for the payment of a full or partial commission to the salesperson who sells his or her broker's own unlisted property. Under these circumstances the division of commissions earned could be other than normal. A provision in the contract also may allow associate licensees to purchase *in-house* listings. The broker may discount all or a portion of the office share of the commission. In addition the contract may contain a reference to commissions owed the employing broker when associates sell their own real property through the office.

Other provisions might be added to this type of contract, depending on the nature of the relationship the parties wish to create. A broker should consult an attorney for assistance in drawing up the contracts to include any or all items suggested in this discussion.

QUESTIONS

1. An agency relationship requiring disclosure is created between a real estate broker and a property owner when:

    a. a licensee activates his or her broker's license under the provisions of Idaho Real Estate License Law.
    b. an unsolicited property owner telephones the broker's office to ask the broker to find a purchaser for his or her real estate.
    c. the property owner signs a written listing agreement employing the broker to find a purchaser for his or her real estate.
    d. the broker introduces the property owner to a prospective purchaser who is ready, willing and able to purchase the property owner's real estate.

2. The amount of a broker's commission in a real estate sales transaction:

    a. must be stated in the listing agreement.
    b. is determined according to the standard rates set by agreement of the local real estate brokers.
    c. if under dispute, will be determined through arbitration by the Idaho Real Estate Commission.
    d. must be paid with cash or a cashier's check upon closing.

3. A broker has met the ultimate test of a listing agreement and will be paid a commission in a real estate transaction when:

    a. a listing agreement has been completed and properly signed by the sellers.
    b. the broker produces a purchaser who is ready, willing and financially able to execute the purchase of the property involved.
    c. a signed purchase agreement by the buyers and sellers is produced by the procuring broker.
    d. there is a completed sale in which the seller has sold the property to a purchaser secured by the broker.

4. A real estate broker may represent and be compensated by both parties to a real estate sales transaction, if he or she:

    a. prior to closing, notifies designated legal counsel of all parties to the transaction about the dual agency.
    b. becomes licensed as a dual agent with the Idaho Real Estate Commission.
    c. complies with the disclosure law and obtains written consent from all parties to the transaction.
    d. is a licensed practicing attorney at law and affirms he or she is working in the best interests of all parties to the transactions.

5. Which of the following situations best produces a tort for which the broker can be held liable?

   a. The purchasers ask about including the washer and dryer in their offer, and the broker replies "I'm sure the sellers are willing to consider incorporating the washer and dryer in the transaction."
   b. The purchasers ask the broker's opinion as to the condition of the roof, and the broker says "It appears to me to be in excellent condition."
   c. The purchaser does not ask, so at the seller's request the broker does not volunteer that there is substantial latent termite infestation.
   d. The seller stated in the listing interview and on the listing agreement that the furnace was new last year, when in fact it needed to be replaced. When asked by the purchaser the condition of the furnace, the listing broker stated, "The seller said the furnace was new last year."

6. Which of the following would *not* be included in a contract between a real estate broker and a salesperson who is an independent contractor?

   a. The salesperson is a subagent only with regard to the broker's clients; he or she is not an employee or partner of the broker.
   b. The broker will make all necessary withholdings from the salesperson's pay, and the salesperson will be enrolled in the broker's group insurance plan.
   c. the salesperson will furnish his or her own automobile and take out an automobile insurance policy.
   d. A statement including the exact amount or percentage of compensation the sales associate will receive for both sales and listing commissions earned.

5

Listing Agreements

THE LISTING AGREEMENT

The Idaho Statute of Frauds, as applied to the real estate broker, sales associate and associate broker, provides that *no contract for the payment of any sum of money or thing of value, as and for a commission or reward for the finding or procuring by one person of a purchaser of real estate of another shall be valid unless the same shall be in writing, signed by the owner(s) of such real estate, or his or her legal, appointed and duly qualified representative.* Furthermore the Idaho Real Estate Commission requires a broker or sales associate who obtains a listing to give the person or persons signing the listing a legible, signed, true and correct copy at the time the listing is signed. This will provide proof that the broker did not alter the contract after it was signed by the seller. Every listing agreement, exclusive and nonexclusive, must state a definite expiration date, a legally enforceable description of the property, price and terms, fee or commission and proper signature. It may not contain a provision requiring the signing party to notify the broker of his or her intention to cancel the listing after the expiration date. The principal needs to know exactly what the salesperson will do for the commission. Open communication and discussion of the listing agreement always will help the broker-principal, salesperson-principal and broker-salesperson relationships.

The listing description should contain enough information so that the property can be located from the description alone. If the seller is married the signatures of both spouses are *recommended* on all listings but are *required* if the seller is dealing with community property. The reason both signatures are recommended is that in a community property state, commingling of community property with separate property is very easy and often cannot be determined accurately without a court opinion.

The listing/employment contract should clarify certain other points. A provision should either authorize or forbid the placement of a For Sale sign and a lockbox, if they are used, on the property. The contract also should provide that the broker will have access to the property at reasonable times to show it to prospective purchasers. The agreement should set a date for the buyer's possession of the premises; in other words, when the seller will be ready to move. In addition the agreement must provide that, if an exchange of property is agreed on, the broker may represent and receive an additional commission from the other party to the exchange. No listing agreement may require the owner to pay any part of the broker's commission in advance or to pay any advertising expenses; however, a seller who desires special advertising for the property must pay for it.

Mobile Homes/Manufactured Housing

The authority of real estate licensees to sell used mobile homes, also known as manufactured housing, without obtaining a special license is provided within Idaho Code 44-2102 and does not restrict the number of used units a licensee can sell. Nor does it require the involvement of either owned or leased real estate.

Section 63-307A of the Idaho Code defines *mobile home* as a structure transportable in one or more sections that is 8 body feet or more in width, 32 body feet or more in length, built on a permanent chassis, designed to be used as a dwelling with or without a permanent foundation connected to required utilities and equipped with plumbing, heating, air-conditioning and electrical systems.

Section 63-307B of the Idaho Code states that a mobile home, as defined above, may constitute real property if the running gear is removed and if the following conditions are met:

a.   The mobile home becomes permanently affixed to a foundation on land that is owned or being purchased by the owner or purchaser of said mobile home. *and*

b.   The owner or purchaser of a mobile home records with the county recorder in the county in which the mobile home will be situated a nonrevocable option to declare the mobile home as real property.

c.   The exercise of said option requires all county assessors to treat those mobile homes whose owners or purchasers have exercised said option as any other site-built residence and shall permit lending institutions to treat said mobile homes as real property or as any other residence.

d.   A mobile home may be considered real property for taxation and financing purposes only and not for any other purposes whatsoever.

Types of Listings

Idaho brokers use open, exclusive-agency and exclusive-right-to-sell listing agreements; the more populated areas use multiple listings. Net listings, as described in the text, are prohibited by some states and not recommended by other states. They are further discouraged in Idaho by the requirement that listings state a fee or commission. However, net listings are not prohibited by Idaho law.

In general the exclusive-right-to-sell listing carries the greatest advantages for both broker and property owner. A broker cannot justify expending time and money on a property if he or she is not assured of a commission (if another broker sells the property). The property owner or seller who gives an exclusive-right-to-sell listing has the right to demand the broker's preferred attention to the property. For this reason a broker should not take such a listing unless he or she believes the property can be sold and intends to give it preferred attention.

The agent with an exclusive-right-to-sell contract is assured of fair compensation and always will be looking out for the seller's best interests. Such a broker can justify the cost of marketing the property, spending the necessary time on it and offering it through other brokers via the multiple-listing service. The seller who gives an exclusive-right-to-sell listing is buying a special service with real selling power—the broker's special attention combined with wide market distribution—and is more likely to get good results quickly.

Listing Considerations

Whereas a real estate listing is the broker's employment contract, it is also the means of securing merchandise to sell. The quantity and quality of the merchandise a broker has available for sale will determine to a great extent his or her success. Because a broker's public image is partly created by the merchandise offered by the agency, he or she has many factors to consider before taking a listing.

Terms. The various factors involved in a real estate sale should be explained to the seller at the time the listing is taken. The seller undoubtedly will be required to pay certain financing and closing costs in connection with the sale and should consider these expenses when deciding on a selling price. Another consideration is the amount and type of loan the buyer will be able to obtain. If a seller makes unreasonable demands regarding price and/or terms after the broker has explained such factors, the broker may wish to decline taking the listing.

Potential. The broker also must consider the buyer appeal that one property has over another. How will the property look to prospective purchasers? Will they realize the property's full potential when they see it? Is it neat and clean? Does it look as appealing as other properties in the neighborhood? Are there too many or too few furnishings? Will the property be accessible at reasonable times for the broker to show it to prospective purchasers? These are a few of the factors to consider when taking a listing. Remember the maxim "A property well listed is half sold." The broker and each salesperson should seek only as many listings as the brokerage can effectively handle, taking the number of sales associates into consideration and emphasizing the quality and not the quantity of listing inventory. Recent court cases across the United States have held that the exclusive-right-to-sell listing creates an inherent duty of *due diligence* on the part of the real estate broker taking such a listing.

Inspecting the Premises

The broker should carefully inspect a property before accepting a listing. If possible, this inspection should be made in the owner's presence. The owner will be impressed with the broker's thoroughness, and the broker can discover any weaknesses in the property that should be considered when deciding on a selling price. The broker also should note any advantages in the property or the neighborhood that will make good selling points. Familiarity with the property will enable the broker to discuss it more intelligently and sell it more quickly. Many sales have been delayed or lost because the broker had inadequate information to answer all of the buyer's questions.

A record should be made of the size of the lot; size, style and age of the house; number of rooms; type and condition of the heating plant; and any other improvements on the property. Conditions of the existing loan, the original price of the property and the amount of cash required by the owner from the sale also should be noted. In other words, the broker should learn as much as possible about the physical and financial aspects of the property. During the inspection the broker may note certain physical changes or improvements needed to effect an early sale. The broker may suggest that the owner make these changes before offering the property for sale.

Taking the Listing

When taking a listing, the real estate agent must get as much information as possible about the property so that all possible contingencies can be anticipated and provided for. The following list suggests subject areas that a real estate agent should explore when taking a listing for a parcel of residential real estate:

1. street address,

2. lot size,

3. age of property,

4. any real property to be removed from the premises and any personal property to be included in the sale (both the listing agreement and the subsequent sales contract should be specific on these points),

5.   proposed possession date,

6.   amount of last year's taxes,

7.   amount of outstanding special assessments and whether they will be paid by the seller or assumed by the buyer,

8.   insurance information including type of policy, coverage, length of policy, expiration date, cost and payment schedule and the agent's name and address,

9.   information on any existing loan, including name and address of lender, balance of loan, interest rate, total monthly payment, the date the next payment is due and whether the payment includes taxes and insurance,

10.   type of heating, air-conditioning and kitchen equipment,

11.   type of title evidence, and

12.   any information on utility costs and irrigation fees.

Later the listing agent should check the county records and any existing mortgage, deed of trust or contract to verify the information given by the seller.

Why does the seller want to sell? Has the owner been transferred to another city? Has the family grown too large for the home? Does the owner have some extra money and want to buy a nicer home? Or do financial problems necessitate lower monthly payments? Are the owners divorcing and need to sell the house for the property settlement? Has there been friction with the neighbors? Perhaps the owner does not need to sell and is simply speculating on the market, trying to make a profit. The owner's reason for selling will determine the extent of his or her desire to sell. In taking a listing, a broker also may identify a prospect who is willing to trade properties or purchase a different property.

Supply and demand. How great is the market demand for a specific type of property? This is important to consider when comparing a parcel of real estate with similar properties. If the supply is great and the demand is low, the property may have to be offered at a reduced price to sell it within a reasonable time.

Price. Real estate should be listed at a price that is close to the market value of comparable property. The buying public is well informed, and a broker will have a difficult time securing a higher price for the property. A seller's asking price is frequently above market value, based on his or her opinion of the property's value or on rumors of the price some other seller in the neighborhood obtained for similar property. The broker must advise the seller in this matter so that the seller can make an intelligent decision when a reasonable offer is made for the property. Many times sellers refuse legitimate offers only later to wish they had accepted.

Sometimes a broker will take an exclusive listing for a property at the owner's inflated price and then make little effort to market the property. This often occurs because the sales associates and/or the broker:

1.   has not learned that improperly priced listings can cause lost revenues, deteriorate company image and give public opinion the wrong message about real estate sales being a profession,

2.   is unable or unwilling to accept the responsibility of telling the seller that the property is priced too high and what marketing problems are created by overpricing,

3.   has the idea that later, when the property doesn't sell, the owner will willingly reduce the price,

4.   wants to prevent another broker from obtaining the listing, and

5.   believes that a listing at any price beats no listing at all.

A potential listing agent will earn the respect of the average seller who has a reason to sell by professionally presenting a well-organized and factual presentation of the realistic marketing value of the property regardless of whether or not an exclusive-right-to-sell listing results.

TERMINATION OF A LISTING CONTRACT

In Idaho the seller can *always* terminate the agency relationship without good cause and the real estate agent then *must* cease to act in the seller's behalf. Whether the seller is contractually liable for damages to the real estate broker is not the issue; that question may be answered through settlement or litigation.

A listing agreement for the sale of real estate may be terminated in any one of the following ways:

1.   performance by the broker,

2.   expiration of the time period as stated in the agreement,

3.   abandonment by the broker if he or she spends no time on it (although the broker may be liable for damages),

4.   revocation by the owner (although the owner may be liable for damages),

5.   cancellation by the broker or by mutual consent of the parties,

6.   death, insanity or bankruptcy of either party,

7.   destruction of the property, or

8.   revocation, suspension or inactivation of the broker's license.

ADVERTISING

The Idaho Real Estate Commission has enacted a series of regulations concerning the advertising of real property by real estate licensees. An actively licensed broker or sales associate, dealing with property owned wholly or in part by the licensee and not listed with a broker, shall disclose clearly in all advertising the fact that the person responsible for the advertising is a real estate licensee. All advertising of listed property must show the name of the listing broker's business and office phone number. No other business name may be used until a proper notice of the change in the business name has been received at the office of the Idaho Real Estate Commission. No advertising may provide any information to the public or to prospective clients that is misleading in nature. Information is misleading when, taken as a whole, a distinct probability exists that it will deceive the persons whom it is intended to influence. All advertising of branch offices must show the same business name as the main office of the broker. Only licensees who are actively licensed by reciprocity in Idaho may be named by an Idaho reciprocal licensed broker in any advertising of Idaho real property.

As these rules show, it is very important for a real estate licensee to check all advertising to ensure that the ads are in compliance with the Rules and Regulations as well as the federal Truth-in-Lending Law, which includes Regulation Z.

Figure 5.1   Employment Contract

EMPLOYMENT CONTRACT

THIS FORM TO BE USED ONLY by members of the National Association of REALTORS		NOTICE TO OWNER DO NOT ALLOW your property to be shown unless the prospect is accompanied by a REALTOR.	

EXCLUSIVE RIGHT TO SELL

The Owner hereby employs the Broker of (Company Name) _____ as the sole and exclusive agent of the Owner to sell or exchange the property described in Item #2 below during the term of this contract and on any additional terms hereafter set forth.

1. **OWNER(S).** The full name of the Owner(s): _____

2. **PROPERTY ADDRESS AND LEGAL DESCRIPTION.** The property address and the complete legal description of the property are as set forth below. If the legal description is omitted, incomplete, or in error, the Broker is authorized to insert, correct or attach the correct legal description of the property.

Address _____ City _____ Zip _____

Legal Description _____

3. **TERM OF EMPLOYMENT CONTRACT.** The term of this contract shall commence _____ 19 ____ and shall expire at midnight _____ 19 ____ unless renewed or extended. If the Owner accepts an offer to purchase or exchange, the term of this contract shall be extended through the closing of the transaction.

4. **PRICE AND ACCEPTABLE TERMS** (Complete all applicable provisions)

Owner agrees to sell the property for a total price of $ _____

NEW FINANCING: ☐ Conventional ☐ FHA ☐ VA Owner agrees to pay loan discount points not to exceed ____% of the loan amount. Owner has been advised that certain inspections may be required.

OTHER FINANCING: ☐ Cash ☐ Cash to existing loan(s). Loan payments ☐ are ☐ are not current. Buyer ☐ will ☐ will not be required to qualify and ☐ will ☐ will not release Owner's liability. Owner is aware that some loans have a recapture provision and Owner may be required to pay additional funds to satisfy such recapture.

☐ Owner will accept a minimum down payment of $ _____ and an acceptable secured note for the balance to be paid as follows: _____

☐ Owner agrees to exchange the property for other property with acceptable terms and conditions. _____
☐ Other acceptable terms _____

5. **BROKERAGE FEE**

a. If Broker or any person, including Owner, procures a purchaser ready, willing and able to purchase, transfer or exchange the property on the terms stated herein or on any other price and terms agreed to in writing, the Owner agrees to pay a total brokerage fee of _____ % of the gross selling price OR $ _____. The fee shall be paid in cash at closing unless otherwise designated by the Broker in writing.

b. Further, the brokerage fee is payable if the property or any portion thereof or any interest therein is, directly or indirectly, sold, exchanged or optioned within _____ days following expiration of the term hereof to any person who has examined, been introduced to, been shown or been offered the property during the term hereof.

c. If Owner, upon termination of this employment contract, enters into an exclusive employment contract to market said property with another Broker, then the time period set out above in Item 5, paragraph b shall not apply and will be of no further force or effect.

6. **INCLUDED ITEMS.** Owner agrees to leave with the premises all attached floor coverings, attached television antenna, attached plumbing, bathroom and lighting fixtures, window screens, screen doors, storm windows, storm doors, window coverings, garage door opener and equipment, exterior trees, plants, or shrubbery, water heating apparatus and fixtures, attached fireplace equipment, awnings, ventilating, cooling and heating systems, built in and "drop in" ranges (but excepting all other ranges), fuel tanks and irrigation fixtures and equipment, all water and water rights, and ditches and ditch rights appurtenant thereto that are now on or used in connection with the premises shall be included in the sale unless otherwise provided herein. Also included: _____

7. **EXCLUDED ITEMS:** _____

8. **CONDITION OF PROPERTY.**   At the time of the signing of this employment contract, Owner has no knowledge of any conditions in need of repair or any latent defects to the property except: _____

Owner agrees to inform Broker of any subsequent defects or any conditions in need of repair that may occur prior to closing.

9. **TITLE.**   The Owner represents and warrants that the Owner has full power and right to sell and convey the property. The Owner agrees to provide good and marketable title to the property at the time of closing, free and clear of all liens, encumbrances or defects. The property is currently encumbered by the following liens not already herein noted: _____ The Title will be conveyed by Warranty Deed unless otherwise agreed to in writing. The individual(s) executing this contract represents and warrants that said individual(s) either is the Owner of the property or has full power and right to enter into this contract and to sell and convey the property on behalf of the Owner. Building or use restrictions general to the area in which the property is located, existing easements, and building or zoning regulations shall not be deemed encumbrances for the purpose of this contract. Owner represents to the best of his knowledge that the property complies with current zoning regulations except: _____

10. **LOCKBOX, SIGN AND ADA COUNTY MULTIPLE LISTING SERVICE, INC. (MLS) AUTHORIZATION**

a. ☐ By initialing this box, Owner directs that a lockbox containing a key which gives MLS Keyholders access to the property shall be placed on any building located on the property. Owner authorizes MLS Keyholders to enter said property to inspect or show the same. Owner agrees to hold Broker harmless for any liability or loss. Owner grants said Broker permission to place a sign on the property.

b. It is understood that Broker is a member of the Ada County Multiple Listing Service, Inc. Owner authorizes Broker to make a blanket unilateral offer of subagency, submit a Property Data Sheet, and submit information regarding the property on this contract for the dissemination through the Multiple Listing Service.

11. **DEPOSIT.** The Broker and any cooperating Broker are authorized to receive a deposit from any prospective purchaser who offers to purchase or exchange the property and shall notify Owner of the receipt of any such deposit. Acceptance of such deposit by the Broker shall not constitute Owner's acceptance of any such offer.

12. **NON-DISCRIMINATION.** Owner and Broker acknowledge that it is illegal to discriminate in the showing or sale of the property on the basis of race, color, religion, sex, handicap, familial status or national origin.

13. **INFORMATION WARRANTY.** Owner warrants that the information provided by the Owner herein and on the Property Data Sheet is true and correct.

14. **GENERAL PROVISIONS.**   In the event either party shall initiate any suit or action or appeal on any matter relating to this contract the defaulting party shall pay the prevailing party all damages and expenses resulting from the default, including all reasonable attorney's fees and all court costs and other expenses incurred by the prevailing party. This contract is made in accordance with and it shall be interpreted and governed by the laws of the State of Idaho. If any action or other proceeding shall be brought on or in connection with this contract, the venue of such action shall be in Ada County, Idaho. All rights and obligations of the parties hereunder shall be binding upon and inure to the benefit of their heirs, personal representatives, successors and assigns.

15. **AGENCY DISCLOSURE**

☐ By initialing this box, Owner confirms that prior written disclosure of agency was provided. Owner has read and understands the contents of the "Agency Disclosure" brochure. All cooperating Brokers shall be representatives of the Owner unless disclosed in writing.
THIS IS INTENDED TO BE A LEGALLY BINDING CONTRACT. IF NOT UNDERSTOOD OWNER IS ADVISED TO SEEK THE ADVICE OF COMPETENT LEGAL COUNSEL.
Execution of this form confirms that the undersigned Owner(s) has (have) executed concurrently herewith a Property Data Sheet and grant consent to inclusion of the information thereon into the Ada County Multiple Listing Service, Inc.
I (Owner) hereby acknowledge I have received and fully understand a complete copy of this contract

Owner: _____ Phone: _____ Date: _____
Owner: _____ Phone: _____ Date: _____
Address: _____ City _____ Zip _____
Accepted: _____ (Broker) BY: _____ (Sub-agent) Date: _____

ADA County Multiple Listing Service/Boise Board of REALTORS®

Figure 5.2   Multiple Listing

Manufactured by
Alexander Clark Business Forms
10801 Emerald Boise, Idaho (208) 322-0611

COPYRIGHT ADA COUNTY MULTIPLE LISTING SERVICE, INC., A SUBSIDIARY OF BOISE BOARD OF REALTORS, INC. ALL RIGHTS RESERVED.

Ada County Multiple Listing Service, Inc.

1. ☐1-Residential ☐2-Residential with Acreage ☐3-Condo/Townhouse ☐4-Mobile Home ☐6-Recreation Land with Home

2. * = Required   LISTING # _____ TRANSACTION # _____

3. *AD _____ _____ *AR _____ *BR _____
   ADDRESS (#)   (STREET NAME)   AREA #   # OF BEDROOMS

4. *LO _____ LIST OFFICE NAME _____ LIST OFFICE PHONE _____
   LIST OFFICE #

5. *LAG _____ LIST AGENT NAME _____ LIST AGENT PHONE _____
   LIST AGENT #

6. *LP _____ *LD __/__/__ *XD __/__/__
   LIST PRICE $ LIST DATE (MM/DD/YY)   EXPIRE DATE (MM/DD/YY)

Coded Fields:

*AGE AGE
☐ A. NEW-INSUL. DISCL. REQ. (NEW)
☐ B. REMODELED (REM)
☐ C. 1-5 YEARS (1-5)
☐ D. 6-10 YEARS (6-10)
☐ E. 11-15 YEARS (11-15)
☐ F. 16-20 YEARS (16-20)
☐ G. 21-30 YEARS (21-30)
☐ H. 30+ YEARS (30+)
☐ I. OLDER (OLD)
☐ J. HISTORIC (HIS)
☐ K. TO BE BUILT (TBB)

*AIR AIR CONDITIONING
☐ A. CENTRAL AIR (CTL)
☐ B. WINDOW UNIT (WIN)
☐ C. EVAPORATIVE COOLER (EVP)
☐ D. OTHER (OTH)
☐ E. NONE (NO)

*AFE ASSOCIATION FEES
☐ A. MONTHLY (MTHLY)
☐ B. QUARTERLY (QTRLY)
☐ C. ANNUAL (ANNL)
☐ D. NONE (NONE)

*BFN BASEMENT FINISHED
☐ A. PARTIAL (PAR)
☐ B. FULL (FUL)
☐ C. NONE (NO)

*CON CONSTRUCTION-HOUSE
☐ A. FRAME (FRM)
☐ B. BRICK/FRAME (B/F)
☐ C. BRICK (BRK)
☐ D. STUCCO (STC)
☐ E. FRAME/METAL SIDING (FAM)
☐ F. LOG (LOG)
☐ G. CONCRETE (CON)
☐ H. STONE &/OR MASONRY (STN)
☐ I. STEEL (STL)
☐ J. OTHER (OTH)

*FLD FLOOR (DOWN)
☐ A. ENTRY (ENT)
☐ B. LIVING ROOM (LRM)
☐ C. FORMAL DINING (FDN)
☐ D. KITCHEN (KIT)
☐ E. EATING SPACE (EAT)
☐ F. FAMILY ROOM (FAM)
☐ G. UTILITY ROOM (UTL)
☐ H. BEDROOM (BDR)
☐ I. MASTER BEDROOM (MBR)
☐ J. NONE (NO)

*FLM FLOOR (MAIN)
☐ A. ENTRY (ENT)
☐ B. LIVING ROOM (LRM)
☐ C. FORMAL DINING (FDN)
☐ D. KITCHEN (KIT)
☐ E. EATING SPACE (EAT)
☐ F. FAMILY ROOM (FAM)
☐ G. UTILITY ROOM (UTL)
☐ H. BEDROOM (BDR)
☐ I. MASTER BEDROOM (MBR)
☐ J. NONE (NO)

*FLU FLOOR-UPPER (UP)
☐ A. ENTRY (ENT)
☐ B. LIVING ROOM (LRM)
☐ C. FORMAL DINING (FDN)
☐ D. KITCHEN (KIT)
☐ E. EATING SPACE (EAT)
☐ F. FAMILY ROOM (FAM)
☐ G. UTILITY ROOM (UTL)
☐ H. BEDROOM (BDR)
☐ I. MASTER BEDROOM (MBR)
☐ J. NONE (NO)

*FPL FIREPLACE
☐ A. ONE (1)
☐ B. TWO (2)
☐ C. THREE OR MORE (3+)
☐ D. INSERT (INS)
☐ E. WOOD STOVE (WST)
☐ F. NONE (NO)

*GAR GARAGE
☐ A. 1 CAR (1)
☐ B. 2 CAR (2)
☐ C. 3 CAR (3)
☐ D. 4 OR MORE (4+)
☐ E. CARPORT (CPT)
☐ F. DETACHED (DET)
☐ G. GARAGE CONVERSION (CNV)
☐ H. ADDITIONAL PARKING (APK)
☐ I. OTHER (OTH)
☐ J. NONE (NO)

*HT HEATING
☐ A. GAS (GAS)
☐ B. ELECTRIC (ELE)
☐ C. OIL (OIL)
☐ D. GEOTHERMAL (GEO)
☐ E. WOOD (WD)
☐ F. FORCED AIR (FA)
☐ G. BASEBOARD (BB)
☐ H. WALL (WAL)
☐ I. CEILING (CLG)
☐ J. HOTWATER (HWT)
☐ K. RADIANT (RAD)
☐ L. OTHER (OTH)
☐ M. NONE (NO)

*KFE KITCHEN FEATURES
☐ A. OVEN/RANGE (O/R)
☐ B. DISHWASHER (DSH)
☐ C. MICROWAVE (MIC)
☐ D. DISPOSAL (DSP)
☐ E. TRASH COMPACTOR (CMP)
☐ F. REFRIGERATOR (REF)
☐ G. PANTRY (PAN)
☐ H. BREAKFAST BAR (BKF)
☐ I. NONE (NO)

*LVL LEVEL
☐ A. SINGLE (SGL)
☐ B. SINGLE W/BASEMENT (S/B)
☐ C. TWO STORY (2ST)
☐ D. TWO STORY W/BASEMENT (2/B)
☐ E. SPLIT ENTRY (SPL)
☐ F. TRI-LEVEL (TRI)
☐ G. MULTI-LEVEL (MUL)

*LCL LIST CLASS
☐ A. CALL BEFORE SHOWING (CBS)
☐ B. CALL FOR INSTRUCTIONS (CFI)
☐ C. MUST ACCOMPANY SHOWING (MAS)
☐ D. EXCLUSIVE AGENCY (EA)

*LSZ LAND SIZE
☐ A. SMALL LOT, UP TO 6000 SQ.FT. (SM LOT)
☐ B. STANDARD LOT, 6000-10,000 SQ.FT. (STD LT)
☐ C. LARGE LOT, 10,000+ SQ.FT. (LGE LT)
☐ D. HALF ACRE (1/2 AC)
☐ E. ONE ACRE (1 AC)
☐ F. 2-5 ACRES (2-5 AC)
☐ G. 6-10 ACRES (6-10)
☐ H. OVER 10 ACRES (OVR 10)
☐ I. CONDO (CONDO)

*PHO PHOTO CODE
☐ A. MLS TAKE PHOTO (TAKE)
☐ B. 1 PHOTO SUBMITTED (1SUB)
☐ C. 1 DIRECTIONAL DRAWING SUBMITTED (1DRW)
☐ D. OTHER (OTH)

*POL POOL/SPA
☐ A. POOL (PL)
☐ B. HOT TUB (HTB)
☐ C. ABOVE GROUND (ABG)
☐ D. IN GROUND (ING)
☐ E. PRIVATE (PRI)
☐ F. COMMUNITY (COM)
☐ G. NONE (NO)

*RF ROOF
☐ A. WOOD SHINGLE (WD SHG)
☐ B. COMP SHINGLE (CMSHG)
☐ C. GRAVEL (GRV)
☐ D. TILE (TILE)
☐ E. METAL (METAL)
☐ F. ROLL (ROLL)
☐ G. OTHER (OTH)

*SWR SEWER
☐ A. YES CONNECTED (SWY)
☐ B. NOT CONNECTED (SWN)
☐ C. SEPTIC (SEP)
☐ D. NONE (NO)

*SHO SHOW INSTRUCTIONS
☐ A. LOCKBOX (LBX)
☐ B. CALL FIRST/USE LOCKBOX (CL/LBX)
☐ C. APPT. ONLY (AP ONLY)

*SIT SITE FEATURES
☐ A. ALARM SYSTEM (A)
☐ B. BARN (B)
☐ C. CABLE TV AVAILABLE (C)
☐ D. CENTRAL VAC (D)
☐ E. COVERED PATIO (E)
☐ F. DOG RUN (F)
☐ G. GARDEN SPACE (G)
☐ H. HANDICAPPED (H)
☐ I. HARDWOOD FLOORS (I)
☐ J. FULLY FENCED (J)
☐ K. PARTIALLY FENCED (K)
☐ L. MASTER BATH (L)
☐ M. MASTER BATH MAIN LEVEL (M)
☐ N. ON CITY BUS ROUTE (N)
☐ O. RV PARKING (O)
☐ P. SHOP (P)
☐ Q. STORM WINDOWS (Q)
☐ R. TENNIS COURT (R)
☐ S. GEOTHERMAL WATER (S)
☐ T. WATERFRONT (T)
☐ U. TITLE TO LAND (U)
☐ V. NONE (N)

*TMS TERMS
☐ A. CASH (CASH)
☐ B. REFINANCE (REFI)
☐ C. CASH OUT/ASSUME (COA)
☐ D. OWNER WILL CARRY (OWC)
☐ E. CONVENTIONAL (CNV)
☐ F. FHA (FHA)
☐ G. 235 ASM (235 ASM)
☐ H. 245 ASM (245 ASM)
☐ I. VA (VA)
☐ J. IDAHO HOUSING AGENCY (IHA)
☐ K. FARM HOME (FRM HM)
☐ L. FHA ASSUME/QUALIFY (FHA/ASM)
☐ M. FHA ASSUME/NO QUALIFY (FHA/NQA)
☐ N. VA ASSUME/QUALIFY (VA/ASM)
☐ O. VA ASSUME/NO QUALIFY (VA/NQA)
☐ P. VA RELEASE ELIGIBILITY (VA REL)
☐ Q. CONVENTIONAL ASSUME/QUALIFY (CNV/ASM)
☐ R. CONVENTIONAL ASSUME/NO QUALIFY (CNV/NQA)
☐ S. EXCHANGE (EXCHANG)
☐ T. WILLING TO SUBORDINATE (SUBORDI)
☐ U. LEASE PURCHASE (LS PUR)
☐ V. CONSIDER ALL (CON ALL)
☐ W. OTHER (OTH)

*WTR WATER
☐ A. WATER SERVICE (WTR SV)
☐ B. SHARED WELL (SHARED)
☐ C. INDIVIDUAL WELL (INDIV)
☐ D. NOT AVAILABLE (NOT AV)

*SPK LAWN SPRINKLERS
☐ A. FULL (FUL)
☐ B. PARTIAL (PAR)
☐ C. AUTO (AUT)
☐ D. MANUAL (MAN)
☐ E. NONE (NO)

7. *CIT _____ *ASF _____ BSF _____ *SOF _____ *CBA _____
   CITY CODE   TOTAL APX. SQ. FT.   TOTAL BASEMENT SQ.FT.   SELLING OFFICE BROKERAGE FEE   COMPENSATE BUYER'S AGENT (Y/N)

8. *TAX _____ *TXY _____ *HOE _____ *LID _____ *UNC _____
   TAXES   TAX YEAR   HOMEOWNER'S EXEMPTION (Y/N)   LOCAL IMPROVEMENT DISTRICT (Y/N)   UNDER CONSTRUCTION (Y/N)

9. *BTH _____ *BAM _____ *BAU _____ *BAD _____ *BM _____ *BU _____ *BD _____
   TOTAL BATHS   BATHS (MAIN FLOOR)   BATHS (UPPER FLOOR)   BATHS (DOWN FLOOR)   BDRMS (MAIN FLOOR)   BDRMS (UPPER FLOOR)   BDRMS (DOWN FLOOR)

10. DPM _____ *GSH _____ *JHI _____ SHI _____ *SUB _____
    DOWN PAYMENT   GRADE SCHOOL   JR. HIGH SCH.   SR. HIGH SCH.   SUBDIVISION CODE

11. *OCC _____ *IRR _____ *FL _____ *SW _____ *ACR _____ *RES _____
    OCCUPIED BY: O - Owner R - Renter V - Vacant   IRRIGATION (Y/N)   FLOOD INS. REQ. (Y/N)   SIDEWALKS (Y/N)   APX. ACREAGE (ENTER FOR RES. W/ACR. ONLY)   (ENTER FOR REC. LAND ONLY) RESIDENCE INCLUDED (Y/N)

12. BUI _____ RNN _____ RPH _____
    BUILDER   RENTER'S NAME   RENTER'S PHONE

13. *LTS _____ ZON _____ ASC _____ APP _____ ATY _____
    LOT SIZE   ZONING   ASSOCIATION FEE $ APPRAISAL $ APPRAISAL TYPE

14. DIR _____
    DIRECTIONS/NEAREST INTERSECTION

15. Dimensions: ENT __X__ *LRM __X__ FDN __X__ *KIT __X__ EAT __X__ FAM __X__ UTL __X__
    ENTRY   LIVING ROOM   FORMAL DINING RM.   KITCHEN   EATING SPACE   FAMILY ROOM   UTILITY ROOM

16. *BDR __X__ __X__ __X__ __X__ __X__
    BEDROOMS

17. Loan #1 LN1 _____ IN1 _____ PM1 _____ OW1 _____
    APX. LOAN $ INT. %   APX. PMT. $ OWED TO

18. P _____ INT _____ T _____ INS _____ ESC _____ ARM _____ AS1 _____ TPL _____
    PRINCIPAL / INTEREST / TAXES / INSURANCE   ESC. TO %   ARM   ASM FEE   TYPE LOAN

19. Loan #2 LN2 _____ IN2 _____ PM2 _____ AS2 _____ OW2 _____
    APX. LOAN $ INT. %   APX. PMT. $ ASM (Y/N)   OWED TO

20. GS _____ JH _____ SH _____
    GRADE SCHOOL NAME   JUNIOR HIGH SCHOOL NAME   SENIOR HIGH SCHOOL NAME

21. *LOC _____ *LEG _____
    MAP LOCATION   LEGAL DESCRIPTION

22. RM1 _____
    REMARKS LINE 1   * NEW CONSTRUCTION ONLY: Required in first line of remarks — CEILING INSULATION: R-Value, Thickness, Type — WALL INSULATION: R-Value, Thickness, Type.

23. RM2 _____
    REMARKS LINE 2

24. RM3 _____
    REMARKS LINE 3

25. RM4 _____
    REMARKS LINE 4

26. RM5 _____
    REMARKS LINE 5

27. OWN _____ OBP _____ OHP _____
    OWNER NAME   OWNER BUS. PHONE   OWNER HOME PHONE

28. 1. Seller(s) have read the foregoing listing form and agree to hold the agent, Boise Board of REALTORS and Ada County Multiple Listing Service, Inc. free and harmless from any liability or damage arising from incorrect or undisclosed information provided by them.

30. 2. Execution of this information form confirms that the undersigned seller(s) has (have) executed concurrently herewith an exclusive right to sell listing agreement with the undersigned REALTOR unless otherwise noted. Seller(s) grant(s) consent to inclusion of the information thereon into the Ada County Multiple Listing Service, Inc.

33. 3. The seller(s) authorization is hereby given if the listing broker wishes to compensate the broker representing prospective purchasers.

34. Seller _____ Date _____

35. Seller _____ Date _____

36. _____ MLS Participant (Broker) or Sub Agent   Date _____   10/25/89

ADA County Multiple Listing Service/Boise Board of REALTORS®

QUESTIONS

1. The type of listing agreement that best assures the seller that the broker will give the property preferred attention and best assures the broker of receiving fair compensation for his or her efforts is a(n):

   a. net listing.
   b. exclusive-right-to-sell listing.
   c. exclusive-agency listing.
   d. open listing.

2. Which of the following provisions is *not* included in the Idaho Real Estate Commission's regulation regarding listing agreements?

   a. A listing agreement must state the exact fee the broker will earn on the transaction.
   b. A listing agreement must be accompanied by a qualified expert's report of the physical condition of the property being offered for sale.
   c. A listing agreement must be in writing and signed by both broker and seller.
   d. The seller must receive a true copy of the listing agreement after signing it.

3. A broker's listings constitute the inventory of merchandise he or she has to sell. When taking a listing, the broker or listing agent should:

   a. consider the local demand for the type of property being offered and whether the specific property being listed has sufficient appeal to attract buyers in the current market.
   b. take as many listings as possible to build up a large inventory of merchandise.
   c. list a property at whatever price the seller desires.
   d. accept a listing without inspecting the property to note its weakness and salable features.

4. Advertisements for real property placed by real estate licensees:

   a. may state only the licensee's box number or street address.
   b. may simply give a telephone number that interested parties can call for information.
   c. must indicate that they were placed in the name of a licensed real estate broker.
   d. must identify the owner of the property being offered.

5. Upon obtaining a listing a broker or licensed salesperson is obligated to:

   a. set up a listing file and issue it a number in compliance with Idaho Real Estate License Law and Rules and Regulations.
   b. notify all other real estate offices in the area that the property is for sale.
   c. cooperate with every real estate office wishing to participate in the marketing of the listed property.
   d. give the person or persons signing the listing a legible, signed, true and correct copy.

6

Interests in Real Estate

ESTATES IN FEE

Freehold estates, as described in the main text, are recognized in Idaho. *Idaho law presumes that a fee simple interest is being conveyed unless expressly stated to the contrary.*

The text also mentions a *defeasible fee estate*, also referred to as a *fee simple qualified. Defeasible* means it is capable of being annulled. Qualifications of ownership are placed on the property by the grantor, who uses language such as "so long as," "while," "during the period," "provided that," "on the condition that" or "if." The type of defeasible fee estate created depends on the particular phrase used. The text divides the defeasible estate into two types: a *determinable fee estate* and a *fee simple subject to a condition subsequent* or *(precedent)*. The owner of the defeasible fee holds the same interest as the owner of the fee simple absolute estate, but the defeasible fee holder's interest may be annulled at some later date if certain events should happen.

The determinable estate carries the limitation that the interest will terminate *automatically* upon the happening of a specific event, and title will revert to the original grantor or that grantor's heirs. (In the case of the *determinable fee subject to an executory limitation* the ownership automatically transfers to a designated third party.) The continued ownership of a fee simple determinable estate is predicated upon certain conditions, which are usually expressed by the words "so long as," "while" or "during the period." Because the courts frown on automatic reversions, they require the use of the above language or a clear expression of intent that the interest automatically reverts. *Example:* Happy Landowner conveys land "to the city of Boise *so long as* it is used for a park and when it is no longer used for a park it shall revert back to Happy Landowner or his heirs."

The fee simple subject to a condition subsequent, on the other hand, is a grant that is to be used for a specific purpose and contains the words "provided that," "on the condition that" or "if." It is similar in that should a breach of the condition occur, the property can revert to the original grantor or the grantor's heirs; however, the reversion is not automatic. The grantor or the grantor's heirs must physically retake possession of the property or exercise their power of termination within a reasonable period of time after the breach. The estate remains with the grantee until the grantor exercises these powers. *Example:* J. A. Jones deeds his property to the city of Ipswitch, Idaho, *on the condition that* the city use the property for a public park. A fee simple subject to a condition subsequent has been created, and if the condition is violated J. A. Jones may exercise his power of termination and end the city of Ipswitch's estate.

He could also have created *a fee simple subject to a condition precedent* in this example and probably would have had he required the city to appropriate the money to build a park in a period of time (for example two years). The transfer of the title to the property would occur only when the condition had been met, even though the document had been prepared and recorded previously.

LIFE ESTATES

The degree, quantity, nature and extent of ownership interest that a person has in real or personal property that is limited in duration to the life of its owner or the life of some other designated person is called a *life estate*. If a life estate, which is *not* an estate of inheritance, is measured by the lifetime of a person other than its owner, it is called a life estate *pur autre vie*. After a life estate is terminated, the estate must do one of two things: revert back to the original grantor (that interest is called a *reversion*) or transfer to a designated third person (that interest is called a *remainder* and the person receiving the remainder is called a *remainderman* or a *remainderperson*). The person to whom the life estate has been granted is called a *life tenant*. The life tenant:

1. is entitled to possession and ordinary uses and profits of the land,

2. is obligated to keep the premises in a reasonable state of repair and free of waste,

3. is to pay ordinary taxes,

4. is barred from creating an interest that extends beyond the measuring life,

5. is under no obligation to insure the premises for the benefit of the future interest holders,

6. may sell or encumber his or her interest and the interest is subject to execution sale if there is a money judgment against him or her, and

7. can give no greater interest to the transferee than the life tenant had at the time of the transfer. *Example:* If Michael deeds his property to Lisa for as long as Rebecca lives and Lisa transfers her interest to John, then John's interest ceases when Rebecca's life terminates.

Legal Life Estates

Curtesy and dower have been abolished in Idaho. Idaho has community property laws. Community property is discussed in Chapter 7 of the text and this Supplement.

Homestead

In 1989 the Idaho legislature made some significant changes in the Idaho Code affecting the homestead exemption. These changes relate to mobile (or manufactured) homes, a change in the procedures necessary to declare a homestead and to an increase in the amount of the homestead exemption. In Idaho a homestead is *an exemption allowed by law against unsecured creditors* and has nothing to do with the homestead as a legal life estate concept that is recognized by many states.

The homestead basically consists of the house or mobile home in which the owner resides or intends to reside and the land on which the dwelling unit is situated. The property actually must be used or intended to be used as a principal home for the owner. If the owner is married the homestead may consist of the community or jointly owned property of the couple or the sole and separate property of either spouse.

The amount of the homestead exemption is the actual net value of the land and improvements to a maximum of $30,000. This maximum amount is after payment of any real estate taxes or special assessments, mortgages, deeds of trust or liens that have an appropriate priority claim.

There are two ways to create the homestead exemption. The first is the automatic nature of the homestead under Idaho Code that occurs from the time the property is occupied as a principal residence by the owner. The second way occurs when the owner selects a homestead from unimproved or improved land that is not yet occupied as a homestead. To create the homestead exemption in the second situation, the owner must execute and file a declaration of homestead in the office of the county recorder in which the land is located.

The conveyance or encumbrance of a homestead of a married person cannot occur unless the instrument by which it is conveyed or encumbered is executed and acknowledged by both husband and wife. The homestead is exempt from attachment and from execution or forced sale for the debts of the owner up to $30,000. Also exempt are proceeds from the voluntary sale of the homestead, in good faith, for the purpose of acquiring a new homestead and the insurance receipts covering destruction of homestead property held for use in restoring or replacing the homestead.

A homestead is presumed abandoned if the owner vacates the property for a continuous period of at least six (6) months. If an owner will be absent from the homestead for more than six (6) months but does not intend to abandon the homestead and has no other principal residence, the owner may execute and acknowledge a declaration of nonabandonment.

EASEMENTS

An easement is a right acquired by the owner of one property to use the land owned by another person for a specific purpose. The various kinds of easements are discussed in the text and all are applicable in Idaho. An *easement by necessity* as described also is known as an *easement by operation of law*.

Easement by prescription. In Idaho a person may acquire an easement by prescription in the lands of another provided he or she has had continuous and uninterrupted use of the land for a period of *five years*. Such use must be open, so that the owner easily can know of it, and it must be hostile; that is, without the owner's permission. The easement acquired by prescription is limited to the exact nature of the hostile use placed on the property by the party establishing the easement right.

WATER RIGHTS

Ownership of water rights in Idaho is determined by the doctrine of prior appropriation, not the doctrine of riparian rights that is described in the text. Under the doctrine of prior appropriation all waters of the state, when flowing in their natural channels, including the waters of all natural springs and lakes within the boundaries of the state, are declared to be the property of the state. The state supervises the appropriation and allotment of water through the Idaho Department of Water Resources. The right to use water for useful or beneficial purposes is recognized and confirmed. The right to use public waters is not considered a property right in itself, but the right becomes appurtenant to the land or other thing to which, through necessity, the water is being applied. The right to continue the water use can be denied only for failure on the part of the user to pay the ordinary charges or assessments that may be made to cover the expenses for the delivery of the water. Prerequisites to appropriation of water are putting the water to a beneficial use and diverting the water from its natural channel or location to the property being benefited.

Private water rights. These are the waters of any lake not exceeding 5 acres in surface area at high-water mark and located or situated wholly or entirely on the lands of a person or corporation in this state.

Permit versus license. Every potential surface water user must obtain a permit from the Idaho Department of Water Resources for the right to use available surface water. After a water permit is given, the permittee has a certain period of time in which to develop the water use and gain a water license. The user holding the oldest recorded water right has the legal right to satisfy his or her needs before anyone else. Then the user holding the next oldest water right has a legal right to satisfy his or her needs from the surplus, and so on, until no surplus remains. No water rights licenses were issued in Idaho prior to 1903.

Perfecting water rights. To perfect (legally establish) water rights, a person must (1) obtain from the Department of Water Resources a permit to appropriate water and (2) put the water to beneficial use by making actual use of the water. A water rights license then is issued. A water permit is personal property and must be transferred by assignment. The transfer of property rights to a new owner *does not* include rights under a water permit. Only when an owner has perfected his or her water rights through a license do the rights become appurtenant to the land on which the water has been beneficially applied. Those rights automatically transfer when a deed has been delivered to a new owner. After a license is issued, it becomes a permanent water right; however, that right can be lost by abandonment of beneficial use for five years.

Groundwater. Groundwater is all water under the surface of the ground. Under the Idaho Code a property owner has certain limited rights to use the water under his or her property for domestic purposes. The term *domestic purposes* does not include land irrigation but does include water for the household and a sufficient amount for the use of domestic animals kept with and for the use of the household. Groundwater other than for domestic use is appropriated by permit in the same manner as surface water.

Percolating water. Percolating water is underground water that is not confined to any set channel or bed. Although the concept of percolating water exists in many states, it is not applicable in Idaho.

Geothermal resources. The term *geothermal resource* refers to the natural heat energy of the earth that may be found in any form and position and at any depth below the surface of the earth. Such resources may result from, be created by or be extracted from such natural heat. and all minerals in solution or other products obtained from the material medium of any geothermal resource. Geothermal resources are a separate class, neither mineral resources nor water resources. They also are closely related to and affecting and affected by water and mineral resources. The geothermal resources of Idaho are under the direction of the Department of Water Resources.

Legal advice. Perfecting, maintaining and using water rights often present complex legal questions. If a question on water rights arises in a real estate transaction, the broker or salesperson should advise clients to seek professional legal advice.

QUESTIONS

1. When Ed McCormack's son got married, Ed deeded the newlyweds a house free and clear of any financial liens. The conveyance included a stipulation that if they should ever divorce, their ownership of the property would terminate automatically and title to the property would pass to Ed's daughter Melissa. Their ownership interest in the property is a fee simple:

   a. subject to a life estate with an estate in remainder to Melissa.
   b. determinable estate subject to an executory limitation.
   c. defeasible subject to a condition precedent.
   d. defeasible subject to a condition subsequent.

2. Anne Janeway conveyed a small farm to her mother for the rest of her mother's life. Upon her mother's death, title to the property will pass back to Anne. Anne's interest in the farm while her mother is still alive is known as a:

   a. dower.
   b. remainder.
   c. executory limitation.
   d. reversion.

3. The homestead exemption granted by Idaho law to a homeowner who is a single head of household is:

   a. $12,500.
   b. $25,000.
   c. $27,000.
   d. $30,000.

4. Proceeds of the voluntary sale of the homestead in good faith for the purpose of acquiring a new homestead shall be exempt for a time period of:

   a. six months.
   b. nine months
   c. 12 months.
   d. No time at all

5. A homestead is presumed abandoned if the owner vacates the property for a continuous period of at least:

   a. three months.
   b. six months.
   c. nine months.
   d. 12 months.

6. In Idaho a person may lose his or her water rights, no matter how they were obtained, by not putting the water to beneficial use for a period of:

   a. three years.
   b. five years.
   c. 10 years.
   d. 15 years.

7. Geothermal resources are the natural heat energy of the earth, in whatever form, and are classified as:

   a. mineral resources.
   b. discrete resources.
   c. water resources.
   d. neither water nor mineral.

8. Which of the following are *not* automatically transferred when the property is sold?

   a. Water rights obtained under a water permit
   b. Mineral rights received but not reserved
   c. An appurtenant easement
   d. An incorporeal hereditament

7

How Ownership Is Held

FORMS OF OWNERSHIP

Chapter 6 in the text and this Supplement describe *what* estates or interests in real estate may be owned. Chapter 7 discusses *how* real estate may be owned. Idaho recognizes the three forms of ownership described in Chapter 7 of the text: ownership in severalty, co-ownership (tenancy in common, joint tenancy and community property) and ownership in trust.

Co-ownership

According to Idaho law a deed of conveyance granting title to a parcel of real estate to two or more persons automatically creates a tenancy in common unless the wording of the deed expressly states the intention to create a joint tenancy or unless the property is acquired as a partnership or community property. Joint tenancy in Idaho does feature the right of survivorship and unity of title, time, interest and possession must be present to create a joint tenancy.

Tenancy by the entirety. Because of the complexity of Idaho's community property laws, this form of co-ownership, as described in the text, cannot be used on real estate owned by a husband and wife as part of their community property. It can, however, be used on property that either spouse owns separately. The owner-spouse can convey the property to both of them on the same instrument with words of conveyance that express the intention of creating a tenancy by the entirety with the right of survivorship and not as community property or some other form of co-ownership. This form of ownership seldom is used in Idaho. Other community property states and many common-law states do not recognize this form of co-ownership at all.

Partition. Any joint tenant or tenant in common may file a suit for partition. If the land involved cannot be partitioned or divided fairly among the co-owners, the court may order the property sold and the proceeds distributed to the former co-owners.

Community Property

In Idaho all property owned by a married person is presumed to be community property until proven that it is being held as separate property. A person's separate property consists of all money and other property owned by him or her before the marriage as well as any such property acquired by gift or inheritance after the marriage. In regard to separate property, each spouse is responsible for his or her own debts, and separate property cannot be appropriated for payment of a spouse's debts. However, community property may be taken to satisfy either spouse's separate debts. In Idaho net income from all separate property during a marriage is considered a community asset.

At any time either before or during a marriage, either spouse may purchase and own property as sole and separate. The purchaser must declare and place in the public record the intention to own this property as sole and separate, so that the law will recognize it as such.

Community property consists of all property and earnings from personal services (in other words, salary) acquired by a husband and wife during a valid marriage. Rents and profits from the separate property of either spouse become part of the community property, especially if commingled or resulting from community effort.

In effect each spouse owns one-half of the community property. Under Idaho law either the husband or the wife has the right to manage and control the community property and either may bind community property, other than real estate, by contract. Neither spouse may convey or encumber real estate held as community property unless the other spouse also joins in (signs) any contract or document involved.

Upon the death of either spouse, one-half of the community property automatically belongs to the survivor and the other half is distributed according to the deceased's will. If the deceased left no will, the other half of the community property passes to the surviving spouse.

Maintaining separate property. Idaho law includes strict regulations on how sole ownership of property can be maintained and legal complications avoided. For example, using community funds to pay the taxes, insurance payments or loan payments for a parcel of separate property could damage that property's sole and separate status. Any real estate salesperson or broker taking a listing for separately owned property should make certain that it is in fact separate property before offering it for sale. A licensee who neglects to check on this fact could be liable for misrepresentation should difficulties be encountered later. Most title companies will require a release of any possible interest by the spouse.

QUESTIONS

1. A deed grants title to a parcel of real estate "to Burt Martin and Robert Jackson. . . ." If the real estate is not being acquired as partnership property, Burt and Robert will acquire title as:

   a. joint tenants.
   b. trustees.
   c. part of their community property.
   d. tenants in common.

2. A married couple's community property includes:

   a. proceeds received as a beneficiary from a non-partnership life insurance policy.
   b. property inherited by either spouse.
   c. wages earned by either spouse.
   d. real estate acquired by either spouse as a gift.

3. Which of the following statements is true concerning community property in Idaho?

   a. Upon the death of either spouse, and if the deceased left a will, all the community property automatically belongs to the surviving spouse, and the deceased's separate property is distributed according to his or her will.
   b. Any real estate that is part of a married couple's community property is held by the husband and wife in a tenancy by the entirety.
   c. Neither spouse may sell any real estate owned as part of their community property unless both spouses sign the sales contract and deed.
   d. Technically, a husband owns two-thirds of a couple's community property, whereas his wife owns only one-third.

8

Legal Descriptions

LEGAL DESCRIPTIONS IN IDAHO

All three types of legal descriptions are used in Idaho. The Government Rectangular Survey System is the base system to which all legal descriptions refer. An acceptable description must use one of the three systems. *A street address by itself is not an acceptable legal description*, which must allow for the determination of the exact size, shape and location of the property.

GOVERNMENT RECTANGULAR SURVEY SYSTEM

All measurements in Idaho are made from an initial point, which is south of the City of Meridian and east of the Kuna Caves. This initial point is approximately 30 miles east, 95 miles north of Idaho's southwestern border.

The Boise Principal Meridian runs north and south at a longitude of $116° 24' 15''$. At the Canadian border on the north, you would be at Township 65 North (T 65 N); Township 16 South (T 16 S) is at the southern border of Idaho. The Boise Principal Meridian passes through the City of Meridian as it goes north from the initial point.

The Base Line, running east and west, passes just south of Boise in the western part of the state and south of Idaho Falls in the eastern part of the state. As you travel across the state in counties like Blaine County, you find a road that is built along the Base Line and is called Base Line Road. *See* Figure 8.1 for the location of the initial point, the Boise Principal Meridian and Base Line as they cross the state.

RECORDED PLATS

Most of the parcels of land within the urban areas of the state are described using recorded plats. Under Idaho Code, if a tract of land is divided into five or more lots, parcels or sites for the purpose of immediate or future sale or building development, except for agricultural purposes, a formal subdivision plat must be approved by the local jurisdiction and recorded by the county recorder. *See* Chapter 19 for a detailed discussion of this process. After the subdivision has been formally approved and recorded, a property then can be described as "Lot 5, Block 2 of Summer Wind Subdivision, Ada County, Idaho." An example of a formally platted subdivision is shown on page 27. On the plat you will find metes-and-bounds descriptions as the lot lines and streets are measured and described. In addition you will find a reference to the township, range and section shown on the face of the plat just under the formal name of the subdivision.

Air Lots—Condominiums

Idaho, like all other states, has enacted a Condominium Property Act. A licensed surveyor will prepare a plat that shows the elevations of floor and ceiling surfaces and the boundaries of the condominium units. These elevations will refer to an official *datum*. Most cities will have an established local official datum that will be used by most surveyors. After the plats have been prepared and approved they will be officially recorded.

METES-AND-BOUNDS LEGAL DESCRIPTION

If a property is irregular in shape and is located in an area where formal platting has not occurred, the property probably will be described using a metes-and-bounds legal description. Another name for this legal description is measurements and boundaries. A survey of the property will be done by a licensed surveyor and a legal description prepared from this survey. The point of beginning (POB) normally will be a section corner or township corner, which directly ties the metes-and-bounds legal description to the government rectangular survey system.

Figure 8.1   Boise Principal Meridian

BOISE PRINCIPAL
MERIDIAN

PRINCIPAL MERIDIAN
- LONGITUDE — 116°24′15″
BASE LINE
- LATITUDE — N43°22′31″

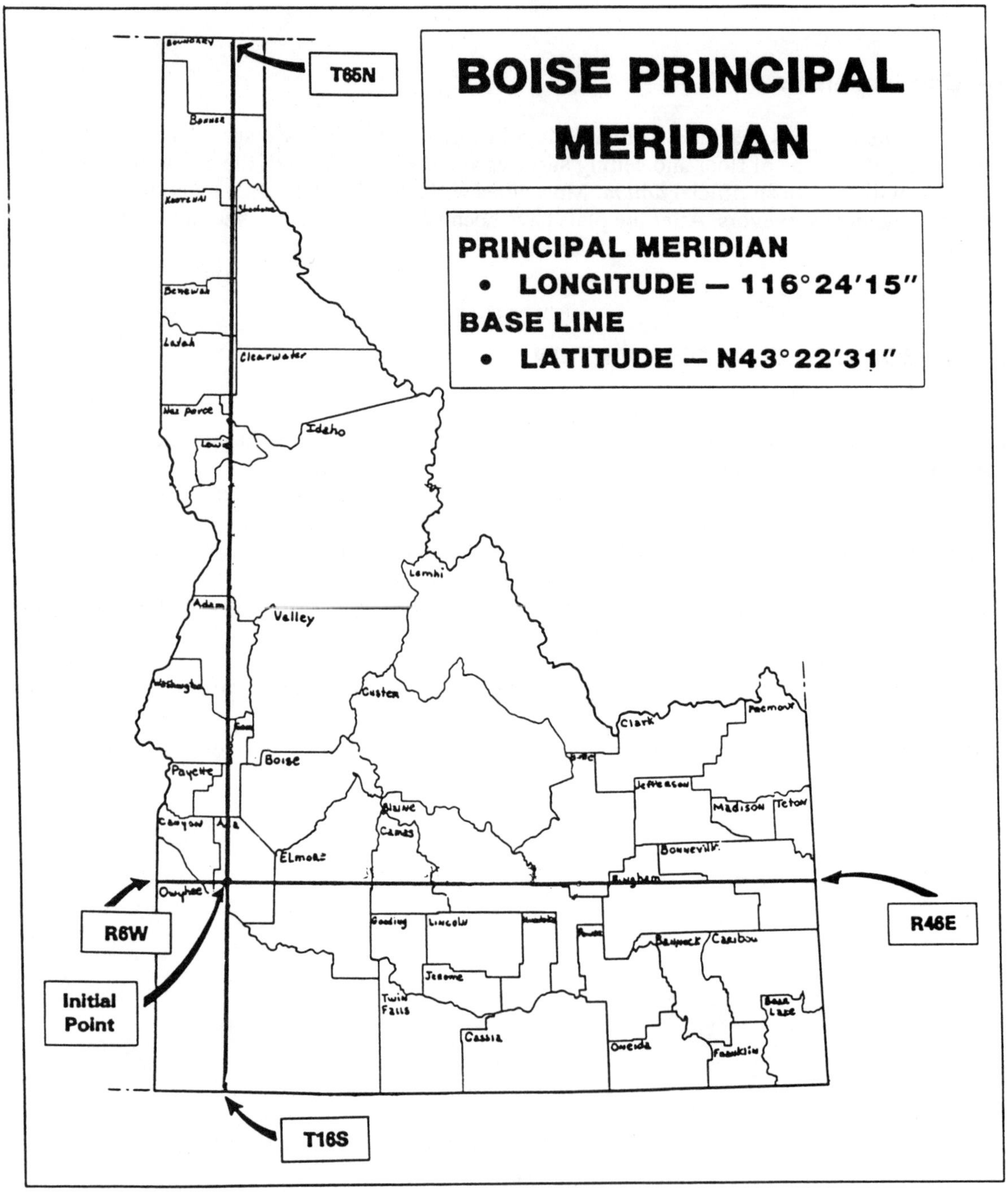

Figure 8.2 High Valley Ranch Subdivision

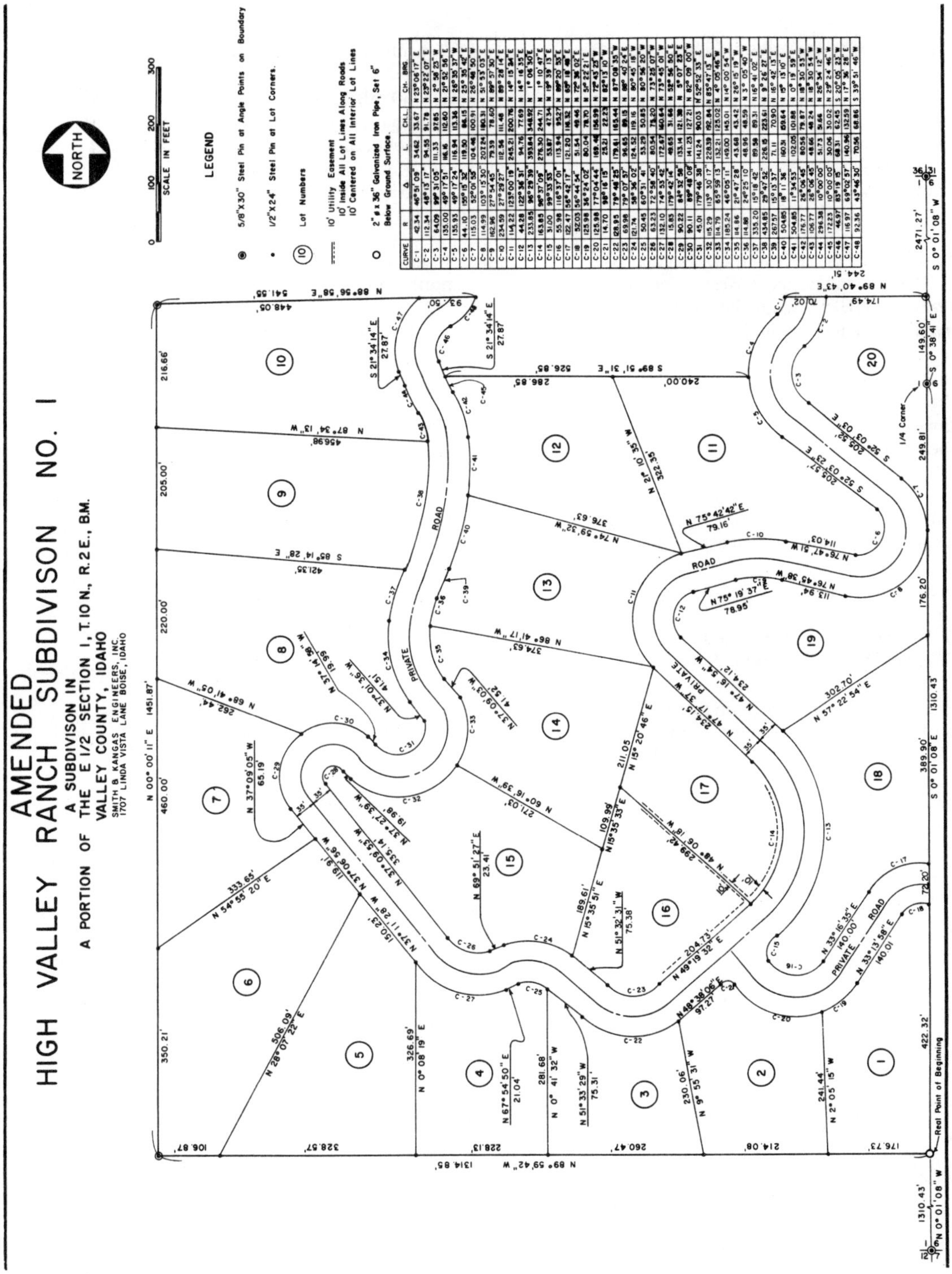

QUESTIONS

1. Which of the following legal descriptions are used in Idaho?

   a. Metes and bounds
   b. Government rectangular survey
   c. Recorded plats
   d. All of the above

2. A property described as the NW 1/4 of Section 10, Township 10 North and Range 2 West of the Boise Principal Meridian (BPM) would be located where in relationship to the initial point?

   a. Northwest of it
   b. Northeast of it
   c. Southwest of it
   d. Southeast of it

3. Which of the following does *not* constitute a proper legal description of a parcel of real estate in Idaho?

   a. Section 12 of T 3 N, R 4 E, Boise Principal Meridian
   b. 6510 Robertson Drive, Boise, Idaho
   c. Lot 5, Block 2 of Summerwind Subdivision, Ada County, Idaho
   d. A metes-and-bounds description that has as its point of beginning the northwest corner of Section 4, T 2 N, R 2 W, Boise Principal Meridian

4. The initial point is located approximately:

   a. 30 miles east of Idaho's western border.
   b. 95 miles north of Idaho's southern border.
   c. south of the City of Meridian and east of the Kuna Caves in Ada County.
   d. All of the above

5. If you were standing at the Canadian border in northern Idaho, the township would be numbered:

   a. T 65 N.   c. T 65 W.
   b. T 65 S.   d. T 16 S.

6. The range number along the eastern border of Idaho would be approximately:

   a. R 26 W.   c. R 46 N.
   b. R 46 W.   d. R 46 E.

9

Real Estate Taxes and Other Liens

REAL ESTATE TAXES

Idaho, like most other states, collects property taxes in order to pay for the costs of local government services. The property taxes are *ad valorem* taxes (a tax on value); the amount of taxes collected is based on the value of the property being taxed.

Assessment

The process of property taxation starts on January 1 of each year. On this date the current taxes for the year become an accruing lien on the property although the actual amount of the tax has not been determined. The county assessor in each county is charged with the responsibility of determining the value of real and personal property for tax purposes.

The State Tax Commission has important responsibility to the county assessors and the county commissioners. The tax commission provides supervision and technical assistance through guidelines and rules and regulations that prescribe the methods used by the county assessor in determining market values for tax purposes. Each year the tax commission does a ratio study that is based on the actual sales prices of real property compared to the market values of real property determined by the county assessor. This study helps establish guidelines for the county assessor.

Between the first day of January and the fourth Monday of June, the county assessor is required to complete all current assessments. Any real property that has been omitted may later be added to the assessment roll. The estimated value must be calculated using the three recognized approaches to value: the *cost approach*, the *market approach* and the *income approach*. If all three approaches are not applicable to the property being valued, then as many of the approaches as possible will be used.

When a property owner believes his or her property has been assessed (valued) unfairly, the assessed value can be appealed to the county board of equalization. The county commissioners sit as the county board of equalization and must meet at least once a month through the fourth Monday of June for the specific purpose of equalizing the assessed value of real property.

In 1980 Idaho passed legislation that eliminated the use of an *assessment ratio*. The terms *market value* and *assessed value* are synonymous. In Idaho the county assessor is required to determine the fair market cash value of property for tax purposes. The assessor also is required to put separate values on the land and on the improvements.

Also in 1980 the legislature passed an *occupancy tax* (Idaho. Code Title 63, Chap. 39). This law provides for a tax on newly constructed buildings until the end of their first year of occupancy. At the start of the following year, such buildings are placed on the regular property tax assessment roll. The law requires the *owner* to notify the county assessor on or before the date of first occupancy. It provides for a penalty of five percent per month for each month after first occupancy, up to a maximum of 25 percent, for failure to report first occupancy. The unpaid occupancy tax becomes a lien on the property.

Mobile homes are assessed in the same manner as other residential housing and are appraised for *ad valorem* taxation. However, the treatment for tax delinquency on mobile homes is quite different from the treatment described for tax delinquency on real property. New mobile homes are subject to the occupancy tax described in Section 63-3901, Idaho Code, just like newly constructed residences and commercial structures.

Property Tax Relief

Exemption for personal residence. The first $50,000 or 50 percent (whichever is less) of the market value of residential improvements is exempt from *ad valorem* taxation if:

1.   The property is the primary residence of the individual applying for the exemption on January 1.

2.   The State Tax Commission has certified to the county commissioners that all the property in the county has been assessed by the assessor. *and*

3.   The owner must apply to the county assessor for the exemption by April 15.

Idaho also allows for certain hardship exemptions and tax reductions. An ordinary exemption for the current year's taxes may be applied for to the board of equalization by a person whose ability to pay the property taxes is affected by unusual circumstances. In addition a person can apply for an extraordinary exemption for delinquent taxes.

A person can apply for a reduction in real property taxes for a personal residence if the claimant:

1.   was domiciled in Idaho the year before a claim is filed,

2.   is over 65 years of age,

3.   is a fatherless minor,

4.   is a widow or widower,

5.   is disabled and meets certain disability requirements,

6.   is a certified prisoner of war or hostage (certification comes from a federal agency), or

7.   is blind.

Besides these requirements, the claimant's total household income must fall within statutory limits. The amount of the tax reduction can range from $50 to $400 or the full amount of the tax, whichever is less. The amount of the reduction will depend on the household income.

Tax Rate

The property tax rate is stated as a percentage of the taxable market value of the property. Every property has a particular tax code area, which is made up of the cumulative tax levies for all the appropriate tax jurisdictions. For example, if the total levies of the specific tax code area are .009875 (0.9875 percent) and the property's taxable market value is $100,000, the taxes would be:

$$\underset{.009875}{\underline{\text{TAX RATE}}} \times \underset{\$100,000}{\underline{\text{MARKET VALUE}}} = \underset{\$987.50}{\underline{\text{TAXES}}}$$

Under Idaho Code (63-923), the maximum amount of all property taxes from all sources on any property cannot exceed one percent of the total market value of the property during any one year.

Tax Statements

The county treasurer is required to send out the tax statements prior to the fourth Monday in November each year. All taxes are paid to the county treasurer and can be paid in either one payment or two equal installments. Payment made as a single payment, must be made on or before December 20. If the taxpayer elects to pay the taxes in two equal installments the first payment is due on December 20, and the second payment is due and payable on or before June 20 of the following year.

Delinquency

If the first half of tax payment is not made by the due date, the taxes become delinquent. A penalty fee of two percent and an interest charge of 12 percent per annum is added to the taxes owed. On January 1 of each year, the tax collector enters the first-half delinquencies on the assessment roll. This entry has the effect of a sale to the tax collector as grantee in trust. If the second-half tax payment is not made on or before June 20 the taxes become delinquent, and the penalty of two percent and interest of 12 percent is backdated to the previous January 1. On or before July 1, the second-half delinquency entries are made (backdated to January 1 in the year the taxes fall delinquent on the roll).

Tax Sale

When property taxes are past due for three years, the county gives notice in the local papers and issues a deed to the property to itself. The property owner may redeem the property after the delinquency and prior to the tax sale by paying all past-due taxes, accumulated interest, penalties and costs. The county will have a tax sale and sell the property to the highest bidder. The county issues a deed to the new owner.

OTHER LIENS

Special Assessments

The procedure outlined in Chapter 9 of the text applies to the way Local Improvement Districts (LIDs) are handled in Idaho. Payments of LID installments are made to the local municipality or taxing district. In many Idaho localities LIDs are not filed or recorded in the county record as are general property taxes, even though they should be.

Mechanics' Liens

Mechanic's lien statutes are provided for those persons who perform labor (including professional services such as surveying and engineering) or who provide materials to use in the improvement of an owner's land or buildings. These groups are entitled to file liens against the property for an amount equal to the value of the labor and/or materials provided.

Any group that finds it necessary to file a mechanic's lien claim must file within an appropriate time. Original contractors (general contractors), engineers and surveyors must file their claims within 90 days of their last day at work. Subcontractors, laborers and materialmen must file within 60 days of their last day at work or after the cessation of providing materials.

The owner of the property must be notified prior to the filing of the mechanic's lien. Within 24 hours of filing a mechanic's lien claim, a copy of the lien must be delivered personally or sent by certified mail to the owner. Mechanics' liens have priority over liens that are recorded after work began on the project. The date of filing of the mechanic's lien does not establish the lien date. The lien date is the date the mechanic started work on the project. Under Idaho's Mechanic's Labor Law Statute, if there are claims by more than one mechanic or materialman and the proceeds are insufficient to pay all claimants, the liens are paid in the following priority:

1.   all laborers, other than contractors or subcontractors,

2.   all materialmen, other than contractors or subcontractors,

3.   subcontractors,

4.   the original contractor, then

5.   professional engineers and licensed surveyors.

In addition if the proceeds are not sufficient to pay everyone the total amount owed, each group will share on a pro rata basis. Idaho does not have a "first in time, first in right" requirement. The lienholder then must file suit to foreclose the lien within six months after filing the notice. If the foreclosure is not filed within this period, the lien will expire.

Judgments

Judgments are effective after they are issued by a court and have been docketed and filed with a county recorder. The judgment becomes a lien only within the county in which it is filed, but a judgment can be recorded in any county in the state. The judgment lien remains a lien against the property for a five-year period. The lien then can be extended for successive five-year periods until action has been taken to collect or enforce the lien.

QUESTIONS

1. In Idaho real estate taxes become a lien on the property on:

    a. January 1.   c. December 20.
    b. June 20.   d. July 1.

2. The Joneses plan to pay the current year's real estate taxes in one payment. To guard against paying a penalty and interest on the taxes, the tax must be paid by:

    a. June 20 of the next year.
    b. December 20 of the current year.
    c. January 1 of the next year.
    d. July 1 of the next year.

3. The Allens will pay the current year's real estate tax in two equal installments. The second-half payment must be made by:

    a. July 1 of the current year.
    b. December 20 of the current year.
    c. January 1 of the next year.
    d. June 20 of the next year.

4. Property taxes in Idaho become delinquent on:

    a. January 1 and December 21.
    b. January 1 and July 1.
    c. June 21 and December 21.
    d. January 1 and June 21.

5. The market value of the Smith home is $125,000. They have filed for the $50,000 or 50 percent exemption on their home. The total tax levy on the property will be .009945. How much real estate tax must the Smiths pay?

    a. $745.88   c. $310.78
    b. $621.56   d. $248.63

6. In problem five, the Smiths decide to pay the taxes in two equal installments. The amount of the first installment will be:

    a. $421.56.   c. $372.94.
    b. $390.78.   d. $103.59.

7. In Idaho a parcel of real estate may be sold for the unpaid real estate taxes when such taxes are delinquent for:

    a. six months.   c. two years.
    b. one year.   d. three years.

8. To claim a mechanic's lien for materials supplied, a supplier must file a notice of the lien in the public record within:

    a. 90 days after the material is supplied.
    b. six months after the material is supplied.
    c. 60 days after the material is supplied.
    d. 90 days after the work is started.

9. To claim a mechanic's lien, original contractors, engineers and surveyors must file a notice of the lien in the public record within:

    a. 90 days after the work is completed.
    b. six months after the work is completed.
    c. 60 days after the work is completed.
    d. 90 days after the work is started.

10. Judgment liens become effective after they are filed with the county recorder. After the lien has been filed, it is effective for how many years?

    a. No set time
    b. Indefinitely
    c. One year
    d. Five years

11. Judgment liens can be extended for how long?

    a. Cannot be extended
    b. One year
    c. Five years
    d. Indefinitely, five years at a time

10

Real Estate Contracts

BROKER'S AUTHORITY TO PREPARE DOCUMENTS

In Idaho it has long been a practice for real estate brokers to prepare some documents by completing or filling in preprinted contract forms, specifically earnest money agreements (specifically purchase and sale agreements) and property listing agreements. When other types of documents are needed, an attorney should be consulted.

The Idaho Real Estate Commission's policy is to prohibit licensees from providing legal advice to either party in a real estate transaction and encourage licensees to recommend that clients consult an attorney when legal assistance is desired or necessary. The Idaho Real Estate Commission's Rules and Regulations specifically prohibit a licensee from discouraging any party to a transaction from seeking an attorney's advice.

CONTRACTS IN GENERAL

Chapter 10 in the text defines a contract as a voluntary agreement between legally competent parties to perform or refrain from performing certain acts for a consideration.

Legal Classifications

Contracts may either spell out specific terms or simply imply them. In an *express contract* the parties state the terms and show their intentions in words, either verbally or in writing. In an *implied contract* the agreement of the parties is demonstrated by their acts and conduct. *Example:* A broker took a listing for a residence and showed the property to prospective purchasers. One serious prospective purchaser told the broker to have a physical inspection made of the property. The broker complied but hired an unqualified person to make the inspection. The purchaser bought the property, discovered a serious physical defect and sued the broker. The court ruled that, although the broker was the agent of the seller, in complying with the purchaser's request the broker had by implication accepted an agency agreement to represent the purchaser. By hiring an inspector who was not competent to do the job, the broker violated a fiduciary duty to the purchaser under this implied agreement.

Contracts also may be classified as either bilateral or unilateral, according to the nature of the agreement. In a *bilateral contract* both parties promise to do something they are not otherwise obligated to do; one promise is given in exchange for another promise. In a typical real estate purchase and sale contract the seller promises to sell and deliver title to a particular parcel of real property to a purchaser, who promises to pay a previously agreed-on amount of consideration for that property. In a *unilateral con-*

tract, or a one-sided contract, one party makes a promise in exchange for an act; that party is not obligated to perform on that promise unless the other party decides to act. *Example:* A homeowner says to you, "If you will paint my house the same color as your house, I'll pay you $1,500." You are not bound to paint the house, nor is the owner bound to pay you. If you should paint the homeowner's house the same color as your house, the homeowner owes you the $1,500.

In addition to these classifications of contracts, a distinction is also made concerning how completely a contract is performed. An *executed contract* is one in which both parties have fulfilled their promises and thus performed the contract. An *executory contract* exists when something remains to be done by one or both parties.

Legal Effect—How Good Is the Contract?

The legal effect of any contract may be described as valid, void, voidable or unenforceable. A *valid contract* complies with all the essentials of a contract and is binding and enforceable on both parties. A *void contract* has no legal force or effect because it does not meet the essential requirements of a contract. For example, a contract to commit a crime is void. A *voidable contract* seems to be valid on the surface but may be rejected or disaffirmed by one of the parties. A contract agreed to under duress is voidable. An *unenforceable contract* is also one that seems on the surface to be valid; however, neither party can sue the other to force performance. For example, a listing agreement is invalid, or unenforceable, unless it is in writing and signed by the parties.

Performance, Discharge and Breach of Contract

Under any contract each party has certain rights and certain obligations. The question of when a contract must be performed is an important factor. Many contracts call for a specific time at or by which they must be completely performed. When no such provision is included, the contract should be performed within a reasonable time. The interpretation of "a reasonable time" will depend on the situation. Generally if the act can be done immediately—such as a payment of money—it should be performed immediately, unless the parties agree otherwise.

Many times, after a contract has been signed, one party wants to withdraw without actually terminating the agreement. This may be accomplished by assignment or novation. *Assignment* refers to a transfer of rights and/or duties under a contract to a third party. Obligations also may be assigned, but the original obligor remains secondarily liable for them (after the new obligor) unless he or she is specifically released from this responsibility. A contract that requires some personal quality or unique ability of one of the parties may not be assigned. Most contracts include a clause that either permits or forbids assignment.

Novation is the substitution of a new contract for an existing agreement with the intent of extinguishing the old contract. The new agreement may be between the same parties, or a new party may be substituted for either of the parties. The parties' intent must be to discharge the old obligation. The new agreement must be supported by consideration and have all the essential elements of a valid contract.

Discharge of contract. A contract may be completely performed with all terms carried out, or it may be breached (broken) if one of the parties defaults. In addition a contract may be discharged (canceled) in various other ways, including:

1.   *Partial performance* of the terms along with a written acceptance by the party for whom acts have not been done or to whom money has not been paid.

2.   *Substantial performance*—one party has substantially performed the contract but does not complete all the details exactly as the contract requires. Such performance may be sufficient to force compliance with certain adjustments for any damages suffered by the other party.

3.   *Impossibility of performance*—an act required by the contract cannot be accomplished; the problem must be with the act itself rather than with the person who should perform it.

4.   *Mutual agreement* of the parties.

5.   *Operation of law*, as in the voiding of a contract by a minor, as a result of fraud or the expiration of the statute of limitations, or as a result of a contract being altered without the written consent of all parties involved.

Breach of contract. The text discusses what happens when one of the parties to an agreement defaults or breaches the agreement and the other party refuses to accept the breach. Certain remedies for such breach of contract are described. The following are some additional remedies available to the injured party to a contract if the other party defaults.

1.   The injured party may waive, or give up, his or her rights to any property given as security by the defaulting party and sue the defaulting party for the balance of the contract.

2.   The injured party may institute legal action to require the defaulting party to pay monies due, or foreclose (cut off) the defaulting party's rights.

3.   The injured party may bring an action to quiet title to remove any claim the other party may have to the property involved, or the party may declare a forfeiture, as described in the text.

Statute of limitations. The law allows a specific time limit during which parties to a contract may bring a legal suit to enforce their rights. Any party who does not take steps to enforce his or her rights within this time period may lose the right to do so. In Idaho an injured party must bring a suit for performance *within five years after the breach of a written contract* and *within four years after the breach of a verbal contract*, as shown below:

IDAHO STATUTE OF LIMITATIONS

Written contract	5 years
Judgment lien	5 years
Adverse possession	5 years
Easements by prescription	5 years
Verbal contract	4 years
Mechanic's/materialman's lien	6 months

IDAHO REQUIREMENTS FOR A VALID REAL ESTATE CONTRACT

The text describes the five essential elements of a valid real estate contract that are applicable to Idaho:

1.   legally competent parties,

2.   an offer and acceptance or mutual assent which includes meeting of the minds,

3.   a legal object,

4.   a legal consideration, and

5.   a written document, signed by all parties to the contract.

Capacity to Contract

Under Idaho law a person becomes of age and has the legal capacity to enter into a valid contract at the *age of 18*. Persons under this age are referred to as infants or minors. Although a minor does not have the legal capacity to contract, he or she may make a contract and live up to it. *A minor's contracts are not void, but they are voidable;* the minor may disaffirm any such contract within a reasonable time after reaching *majority* (the legal age of 18). A minor who is not under the care of a parent or guardian, however, generally is held responsible for contracts to purchase items considered necessities. A married minor may enter into contractual agreements and can sue or be sued. A contract entered into by such a person, however, could be ruled invalid by the courts if it is contested (challenged).

Married women. Under the common law, married women did not have the capacity to contract and their contracts were void. In Idaho, as in most states, this limitation no longer exists. A married woman can enter into a valid contract and she can sue or be sued.

Insane persons. Any contract is void if made by a person who has been declared by a court to be of unsound mind. Such persons must be sufficiently deranged so that they do not comprehend that they are making a contract or what the resultant consequences or obligations will be.

Felons. Under Idaho law a contract entered into by a person who is imprisoned for committing a serious crime (felony) is void, unless such a person has obtained express permission from the state parole board.

Statute of Frauds

The Idaho Statute of Frauds, recently defined by the Idaho Supreme Court as it pertains to real estate transactions, provides that *agreements for the sale of real property, or of an interest therein, and leases of real property for a period of more than one year are unenforceable unless the sale or lease agreement or some note or memorandum thereof, is in writing and signed by both parties*. The Idaho Statute of Frauds likewise limits the effective transfer of any interest in real property, such as liens, easements or rights-of-way, other than by operation of law. Disputes involving the statute of frauds are almost always complex. The above general description of the law is cited so that real estate licensees will be aware of its provisions. In reality, certain exceptions may take a particular transaction out of the operation of the statute of frauds. An attorney should be consulted when a broker or salesperson suspects that a statute of frauds problem may exist.

An agreement to pay an individual money or other valuable consideration for finding a purchaser for another person's property is not valid and enforceable unless the agreement is in writing and signed by the owners of the real estate or their legal representative.

CONTRACTS FOR THE SALE OF REAL ESTATE

Chapter 10 of the text includes a basic discussion of real estate sales contracts. In Idaho such a contract is known as a real estate purchase and sale agreement. The document appearing in Figure 10.1 contains the provisions of the sale in addition to a receipt for the purchaser's earnest money deposit. The Idaho

Real Estate Commission requires that the actual amount of money received by the broker as a deposit and the form of payment (check, note, car title, etc.) be specifically stated in the agreement.

Clauses in the Contract

The actual contents of a real estate purchase and sale agreement and receipt for earnest money may vary from office to office and form to form. The Idaho Real Estate Commission does not require that any particular form be used; however, it does recommend the use of good, standard forms that have been especially designed for selling specific types of property. The form in general use in Idaho is included in this chapter, as noted. As you read the following discussion on the divisions or clauses in a real estate purchase and sale agreement and receipt for earnest money, try to locate the various provisions in the actual contract form.

Date. Every contract must indicate the actual date of the offer.

Purchasers' names. The purchasers' names must be written out as they will appear on all legal documents. If the purchasers are husband and wife, that fact should be noted. If there is only one purchaser, his or her marital status should be indicated.

Receipt of earnest money. The amount of earnest money accepted by the broker should be sufficient to compensate the seller if the contract is not consummated and the sale is not completed. This amount should be written out in words as well as figures. The receipt or earnest money provision also must indicate whether the deposit was cash, a personal check, a promissory note or some other form of payment in lieu of cash. If the manner of payment is not indicated, the seller can assume that the deposit was made in cash; should the buyer forfeit the deposit, the seller then may demand the money in cash (unless the contract provides otherwise). If the buyer will deposit additional earnest money, the contract should provide a definite date for such payment. In addition, the agreement must provide for a division of the earnest money (including any portion paid to the broker) in the event that the transaction is not completed and the earnest money is forfeited.

Adequate legal description. The definite description given must be sufficient for the property to be located from the description alone.

Real property excepted. Most purchase and sale agreement forms include a paragraph listing articles that are part of the property and are to be included in the sale. If the seller plans on removing any of these fixtures, this intention should be written into the agreement to avoid misunderstandings between the parties.

Personal property. Most contract forms also include a paragraph in which any items of personal property included in the sales price may be listed and described. If this provision is acceptable to the buyer, a separate bill of sale for the personal property should be made out when the transaction is closed.

Sales price and terms. The agreement should set forth the full sales price and describe the manner in which it will be paid. The contract will not be binding unless the terms of payment are specifically stated. If the buyer must obtain financing, a brief description of the type of loan, its amount and the amortization period should be included so that the seller will know what kind of financing the buyer is planning to obtain. If the buyer will assume an existing loan, the terms of that loan—approximate balance, interest rate, due date, monthly payments and who will pay any costs to assume the loan—should be clearly specified. If the buyer is asking the seller to carry a contract (installment contract or contract for deed) as part of the purchase price, the following items concerning the amount and manner of payment of the contract must be specified:

1. the amount owing on the contract,

2. interest rate,

3. date interest is to begin,

4. amount of monthly payments and date due,

5. date the first payment is due,

6. who is to pay the escrow filing fee, escrow collection fee and escrow closing fee,

7. who, or what entity, will be the responsible custodian of the escrowed documents,

8. any prepayment penalties or restrictions (if applicable), and

9. whether the property can be transferred subject to the indebtedness, or whether or not there is a due-on-sale clause.

It is dangerous to assume that the parties will understand the contract, unless *all* conditions are set forth in clear and concise language. If additional space is necessary the broker may use the back of the contract form or a separate sheet of paper. Any added pages or writings must be signed by all parties to the agreement.

Other conditions. Any additional conditions or concessions requested by the buyer, such as repairs to the property, should be clearly set forth in the agreement to ensure that the seller understands them.

Encumbrance clause. This section of the contract includes what is described in the text as the "subject to" clause; each contract form has its own wording. Basically, the seller agrees to furnish title evidence that his or her property is free and clear of all liens and encumbrances except any named that will remain outstanding against the property, such as mortgages, trust deeds, leases, easements or restrictions. These must be stipulated in the agreement.

Conveyance and prorations. The contract should state the type of conveyance or deed the seller will deliver to the purchaser. Real property usually is conveyed by warranty deed unless otherwise stipulated (*see* Chapter 11 in the text). Real property is never conveyed by an abstract of title or by a title insurance policy.

All taxes, assessments, rents, insurance, mortgage interest or contract indebtedness should be prorated to the date of possession or any other date that is agreeable to the seller and buyer. If a definite date can be established, it should be made part of the contract.

Performance. The performance clause usually stipulates that the seller must accept the offer and sign the agreement within a specified period of time and that the seller's title to the property must be merchantable and insurable. If the conditions are met and the purchaser then neglects or refuses to complete the sale, the contract provides that the earnest money is forfeited to the seller as *liquidated damages*, or the seller may take legal steps to enforce his or her rights under the contract.

Damage to property. Most contract forms provide that if the property is destroyed or materially damaged before the sale is consummated, the agreement, at the purchaser's option, becomes null and void and the earnest money is to be returned to the purchaser. This clause reminds the seller to keep the property in good condition and repair until the transaction is closed and the buyer has taken possession. It also provides for the possibility of damage to or destruction of the property by forces such as wind, fire or flood.

Possession. The agreement always should state a definite date of possession. In determining a possession date, the broker and the parties to the agreement must take many factors into consideration. How much time does the purchaser need to arrange for financing? When must the purchaser vacate his or her premises? When can the seller move into new premises? To avoid any misunderstandings, the buyer and seller should agree on the best possible possession date and include that date as a provision of the agreement.

Independent investigation. The agent is responsible for making certain that all details of the sale are written into the agreement and are completely understood by both parties. Any verbal agreements pertaining to the sale that are made at any time during the negotiations or before the sale is closed can only cause problems. The agreement should clearly state that the purchaser enters into the contract upon his or her independent investigation and judgment and that no additional agreements, verbal or otherwise, affect the written contract.

Time is of the essence. This clause prevents either party from unjustly delaying the closing of the transaction. The phrase "time is of the essence" means that one party must perform his or her obligations within the time specified in the contract in order to be able to require performance from the other party.

Purchaser's signature. In the final clause, the purchaser(s) agrees to pay a stipulated price for the property under the terms and conditions set forth in the contract, and then signs the offer.

Seller's acceptance. The seller(s) agrees to sell and convey the property under the terms and conditions of the contract and to pay the agent's stipulated commission. When the seller signs the agreement and accepts the offer, it becomes binding on both parties. The earnest money is held in trust by the broker until the closing, when it becomes the property of the seller.

Notary acknowledgment. An acknowledgment is a form of declaration made voluntarily by a person who is signing a formal written document before a notary public. All receipt and agreement to purchase forms used in Idaho should have provision for a certificate of acknowledgment of the seller's signature (*see* Chapter 11 in the text). Because Idaho is a community property state, whenever the sellers in a transaction are husband and wife, both must sign the agreement and both signatures must be acknowledged, or proven. An acknowledgment prevents the possibility of forged signatures on the contract and safeguards against incompetent parties signing the contract. The acknowledgment provides evidence that the signature is genuine. The notary public who has a beneficial interest in a document cannot act as a notary to the same document.

Disclosure provision

Agency disclosure, previously discussed in Chapter 4, must also be made in accordance with Rule 4,4,5 of the Rules and Regulations of the Idaho Real Estate Commission.

Broker's Responsibility

It is part of the agent's fiduciary duty to make certain that the seller understands all the terms and conditions of the contract; the agent's responsibility also includes explaining the contract's provisions to the buyer. When both parties understand the implications of the agreement, the likelihood of misunderstandings, dissatisfaction or withdrawal by either party diminishes.

Idaho law makes the agent responsible for the content of the contract as well. The broker or salesperson must make certain that all the terms and conditions of the sale are included in the contract. The law also provides that, upon accepting an earnest money deposit and a signed offer to purchase from a prospective purchaser, the agent must give that purchaser a copy of the agreement as a receipt. Furthermore, the agent promptly must convey every written offer to purchase to the seller and, upon the seller's acceptance, deliver to each party a true copy of the contract signed by both buyer and seller.

In practice, the person making an offer to purchase should sign the original and at least four copies of the contract. One copy is retained by the purchaser as a receipt; the original and the other three copies are presented to the seller. Upon accepting the offer, the seller signs the original and the three copies. The seller keeps one copy. One copy is given to the purchaser and the other copy and the original are retained by the broker.

Alterations in the Contract

The negotiating process in a real estate transaction involving offers and counteroffers is described in the text. If the seller wishes to make any changes in the contract, the best practice is to fill in a new counteroffer form according to the seller's proposed terms and have both parties sign this agreement.

Out-of-Town Seller

The proper signature from an out-of-town seller is essential. While the broker is waiting for the purchase and sale agreement to make its rounds through the mail, an additional precaution can be taken. After an offer is made to purchase the property of an out-of-town seller, a facsimile (fax) of the original offer or a telegram describing the *exact* terms of the offer immediately should be sent to the seller with a request for a return accepted or rejected fax or a telegram of acceptance or rejection. The broker should retain for the record a copy of the fax or telegram containing the offer and a copy of the reply. If the offer is rejected and no further action is taken by either party, the fax or telegram should be attached to the original purchase and sale agreement, dated and marked "rejected" and placed in the broker's rejection file. If the offer is accepted, the fax or both telegrams (one from the seller and one from the broker) should be attached to the original purchase agreement. As of this writing facsimiles of legally binding agreements or instruments have not been tested in Idaho courts as to their lawful substitution for originals, even through the necessary signatures are notarized on-site. Until there is some ruling it would be wise to treat a fax as you would a telegram.

Double Contracts

Section 4, 3, 0, of Idaho's Rules and Regulations, more thoroughly discussed in Chapter 13, prohibits real estate brokers and salespeople from using double contracts.

In Idaho real estate brokers and salespeople are prohibited from using double contracts. A *double contract* refers to two separate contracts or loan applications concerning the same parcel of real estate, one stating the true purchase price and the other stating a larger amount as the purchase price. Such contracts are used to induce a lender to make a mortgage loan commitment for a larger amount based on the false, inflated purchase price quoted on the second contract. This fraudulent activity represents a "flagrant course of misconduct. . . constituting dishonorable or dishonest dealing" and could result in the suspension or revocation of an agent's license.

HANDLING EARNEST MONEY DEPOSITS (TRUST ACCOUNTING)

The Rules and Regulations addressed in Chapter 13 set forth specific requirements for the handling of earnest money deposits and other funds entrusted to a real estate broker.

The Rules and Regulations set forth specific requirements for the handling of earnest money deposits and other funds entrusted to a real estate broker. Failure to account for trust funds properly, no matter what the reason, is grounds for suspension or revocation of the broker's license. In the interest of the broker's fiduciary obligations, he or she must deposit all funds received from and belonging to others on or before the next banking day, unless directed in writing by the parties to do otherwise. The deposit must go to a neutral escrow depository or in a special trust checking account that is maintained in an Idaho bank. When a salesperson receives these funds, they must be turned in to the broker at once for deposit.

The trust account must be identified with the broker's business name, address and the phrase "Real Estate Trust Account," to distinguish it from any other accounts the broker may have. A broker may have more than one trust account; however, it is best if each account is maintained in a different banking institution. In no case shall entrusted funds be commingled with funds of a real estate broker or salesperson.

Brokers are required to keep all documents and records pertaining to a real estate transaction on file for at least three years after the year in which the transaction was closed. In addition, certain records must be kept concerning a broker's trust account. This will be discussed in detail in Chapter 13 of this Supplement.

The Idaho Real Estate Commission does not intend to dictate a specific record-keeping system. Any system that properly accounts for trust funds and is approved by the commission may be used. In addition, the commission staff is available to help a broker set up an adequate record-keeping system.

Trust account audits. The commission or its representative may make periodic inspections of a broker's trust account to ensure that the broker is complying with all regulations and keeping accurate and adequate records.

OPTIONS

The text includes a discussion of options to purchase or lease real estate. Usually an option gives the optionee an exclusive right to purchase or lease the property in question. Some options, however, grant the optionee the right of first refusal (the first chance) to purchase or lease the property when it becomes available for sale or lease.

Frequently an option will be given in connection with a lease; the optionee leases the property with the option to purchase it at a specified price. Such an option clause usually terminates when the lease expires; if the lease is renewed, the option may be renewed as well.

EARNEST MONEY PROBLEM

Complete the earnest money form (purchase and sale agreement) found in Figure 10.1 of this Supplement according to the facts given in the following description of a real estate transaction:

Data. On September 1, 1990, Mark and Sarah Swenson finally found a home, located at 1313 Honey Locust Drive, Boise, Idaho, that met all of their qualifications and expectations. They had associated themselves with a fine young salesperson named Frank Livermore. Frank was a new sales associate with Gold Carpet Realty, a firm whose owner/broker was his father, Sam Livermore.

The home the Swensons wanted to purchase was listed by Wilson, Wagner & Bills, a member of the local MLS. The listed price was $94,000. The home had an assumable VA loan of approximately $63,100, payable at $582.48 per month including interest at 10.25 percent per annum *plus* reserve payments of $121.52. The sellers wanted cash. The lender, Home and Farm Savings and Loan, charges a one percent assumption fee on the unpaid principal balance, which is to be paid by the purchaser. All of Wilson, Wagner and Bills's listings pay a seven percent commission, one-half of which goes to the selling office in a cooperating sale.

The Swensons decided to make an $87,500 offer on the property the next day with the stipulation that the sellers, Jeff and Ronna Graham, carry back a second trust deed of $8,900 payable in annual payments of $1,500 plus interest at 10.5 percent per annum; the first payment would be due October 15, 1990, with any remaining unpaid balance due in five years. The escrow is to be collected by First Title Insurance Company's long-term escrow department and all fees will be split equally. Their offer was accompanied by a cashier's check of $1,000 made payable to First Title Insurance Company's escrow closing account. The buyers stipulated that the title insurance be provided by First Title Insurance Company. The buyers wanted the sellers to include their new washer and dryer plus a one-year-old window air-conditioner in the sale and also give possession on the closing date of October 15, 1990. All prorations would be to the date of closing.

On September 9, 1990, after several days of hard negotiation, the buyers and sellers came to an agreement. The purchase price was $87,500, and the owners agreed to the second trust deed. But the buyers would assume the sewer LID, which had an outstanding balance of $2,400 plus interest at 9.25 percent per annum, and pay an additional $625 at closing for the seller's personal property. The buyers gave the sellers until midnight to accept their offer. The buyers and sellers also agreed to share equally all closing costs and any inspection fees required by the city or county. (*Note*: The property is in the city, on city sewer and water, and there are no violations of City Code. The legal description is Lot 13 Block 3 of the Randolf Addition to Boise, book 10 page 12 of Plats, Ada County, Idaho.) Check your solution with the one given in the Answer Key for this Supplement.

Figure 10.1   Real Estate Purchase and Sale Agreement and Receipt for Earnest Money

REAL ESTATE PURCHASE AND SALE AGREEMENT AND RECEIPT FOR EARNEST MONEY
(This form to be used ONLY by members of the National Association of REALTORS)

This contract stipulates the terms of sale of the property. Read carefully before signing (including information on reverse side). This is a legally binding contract. IF YOU HAVE ANY QUESTIONS, CONSULT YOUR ATTORNEY BEFORE SIGNING.

_____, Idaho _____ 19 _____

(hereinafter called "Buyer") agrees to purchase, and the undersigned Seller agrees to sell the following described real estate hereinafter referred to as "premises"

commonly known as _____

City of _____ County of _____, Idaho legally described as: _____

(A FULL AND COMPLETE LEGAL DESCRIPTION MUST BE INSERTED, ATTACHED OR WRITTEN ON THE REVERSE HEREOF PRIOR TO EXECUTION BY SELLER. Buyer hereby authorizes broker to insert over his signature the correct legal description of the premises if unavailable at the time of signing, or to correct the legal description previously entered if erroneous or incomplete.)
EARNEST MONEY.
(a) Buyer hereby deposits as earnest money and a receipt is hereby acknowledged of _____ dollars

($_____) evidenced by: ☐ Cash ☐ Personal Check ☐ Cashiers Check ☐ Note Due ☐ or _____

(b) Earnest Money to be deposited in trust account upon acceptance by all parties and shall be held by ☐ Listing Broker ☐ Selling Broker ☐ Other _____

_____ for the benefit of the parties hereto, and _____ (Broker) shall hold the completely executed broker's copy of this agreement and is responsible for the closing.

(c) If all conditions have been met by Buyer, Buyer and Seller agree that the earnest money (less credit report fees, and any other Buyer's costs) shall be refunded to Buyer in the event the financing contemplated herein by Buyer is not obtainable.

(d) The parties agree that _____Title Company shall provide said title policy and preliminary report or commitment and the "closing

agent" for this transaction shall be _____ . If a long-term escrow / collection is involved, then the escrow holder shall be

_____

1. **TOTAL PURCHASE PRICE IS** _____ DOLLARS ($_____)
   payable as follows:

   a. $_____ Cash down, including above Earnest Money (Closing costs are additional).

   b. $_____ Balance of the purchase price (M.I.P. not included).
2. **FINANCING.** This agreement is contingent upon Buyer qualifying for:

   ☐ FHA ☐ VA ☐ Conventional ☐ IHA. Purchase loan balance as noted above for a period of _____ years at _____ % per annum. (If FHA or VA loan is sought, read the applicable provisions on the reverse side hereof.) Buyer shall pay no more than _____ points plus origination fee if any. Seller to pay only the discount points necessary in order to obtain above described financing but not to exceed _____%.

   ☐ Buyer to ASSUME and ☐ will ☐ will not be required to qualify for an EXISTING LOAN(S) of approximately $_____ at no more than _____% with monthly payments of approximately $_____ P ☐ I ☐ T ☐ I ☐. This agreement ☐ is ☐ is not contingent upon Lender releasing Seller's liability.

   Type of loan _____ . Buyer shall apply for such loan or assumption within three (3) banking days after Seller's acceptance of this agreement.
   OTHER FINANCING, TERMS & CONDITIONS: _____

   _____

   _____

   _____

   _____
3. **THIS AGREEMENT** ☐ is ☐ is not **CONTINGENT** upon sale and closing of _____ on or before
   _____ listed with _____
   (If a contingency is noted please read applicable conditions in Paragraph # 15 on reverse side. NOTE: Any waiver by the Buyer under this section will be a waiver of ALL contingencies, including financing.)
4. **ITEMS SPECIFICALLY INCLUDED IN THIS SALE** (if FHA / VA financing is sought see Item # 14 on reverse side): _____

   _____
5. **ITEMS SPECIFICALLY EXCLUDED IN THIS SALE:** _____
6. **COSTS PAID BY:** Costs in addition to those listed below may be incurred by Buyer and Seller. Unless otherwise agreed herein, or provided by law or required by lender, Buyer shall purchase Seller's reserve account if loan assumption.

   ☐ Yes ☐ No. Purchaser's Extended Coverage Title Policy requested. Additional premium paid by _____ . See item # 17 on reverse side.

   If requested by lender or otherwise stated herein, the below costs will be paid as indicated.

Costs Paid By	Appraisal	Loan Assumpt.	Well Inspect.	Pump/Inspect Septic	City/County Code Inspect. if required	Contract and/or Document Prep.	Closing Agent's Fee	Long Term Escrow Fees	Lender or Code Repairs	
BUYER										
N/A										
SELLER										
SHARE EQUALLY										

   Cost of lender or code repairs not to exceed $_____ . Discount points to be paid as agreed on line 29 and 30. *SELLER UNDERSTANDS that as a result of any city or county inspections HE MAY BE REQUIRED TO MAKE REPAIRS to the property in order to comply with the housing code WHETHER OR NOT A SALE IS COMPLETED UNDER THIS AGREEMENT.*
7. **POSSESSION.** Buyer shall be entitled to possession on ☐ closing ☐ other _____ . "Closing" means the date on which all documents are either recorded or accepted by an escrow agent and the sale proceeds are available to Seller. Taxes and water assessments (using the last available assessment as a basis), rents, insurance premiums, interest and reserves on liens, encumbrances or obligations assumed and utilities shall be pro-rated as of _____ . Buyer shall pay for fuel in tank, amount to be determined by the supplier at Seller's expense.
8. **CLOSING.** On or before the closing date, Buyer and Seller shall deposit with the closing agent all funds and instruments necessary to complete the sale. The closing date shall be no later than _____
9. **ACCEPTANCE.** Buyer's offer is made subject to the acceptance of Seller on or before 12:00 o'clock midnight of _____ . If Seller does not accept this agreement within the time specified, the entire Earnest Money shall be refunded to Buyer on demand. Seller's counter offer (if any) is made subject to the acceptance of Buyer on or before 12:00 o'clock midnight of _____ . TIME IS OF THE ESSENCE OF THIS AGREEMENT.
10. **IMPORTANT – AGENCY DISCLOSURE.** At the time of signing this agreement the agent working with the buyer represented _____ and the agent working with the seller represented _____ . Each party signing this document confirms that prior written disclosure of agency was provided to him / her in this transaction. Each party to this transaction has read and understands the contents of the agency disclosure brochure previously received.

Listing Agency: _____ Selling Agency: _____

By: _____ Phone: _____ By: _____ Phone: _____

Buyer: _____ Buyer's Address: _____

Buyer: _____ Buyer's Phone: Residence _____ Business _____

On this date, I / We hereby approve and accept the sale set forth in the above agreement and agree to carry out all the terms thereof on the part of the Seller and the undersigned further agrees to pay a total brokerage fee of _____ to the above named Broker(s) for services. Brokerage fee will be paid in cash unless otherwise agreed in writing.

I / We further acknowledge receipt of a true copy of this agreement signed by both parties.

Seller: _____ Date: _____ Seller's Address: _____

Seller: _____ Date: _____ Seller's Phone: Residence _____ Business _____

A true copy of the foregoing agreement, signed by the Seller and containing the full and complete legal description of the premises, is hereby received on this _____ day of _____ , 19 ____

Buyer: _____ Buyer: _____

THE PROVISIONS CONTAINED ON THE REVERSE SIDE OF THIS PAGE SHALL ALSO CONSTITUTE PART OF THE AGREEMENT OF THE PARTIES. EACH OF THE PARTIES ACKNOWLEDGES READING THIS AGREEMENT IN FULL.

Buyer's initial _____ Seller's initial _____   **BROKER'S COPY**   RE 21 REV. 2/90

Figure 10.1 Real Estate Purchase and Sale Agreement and Receipt for Earnest Money (Continued)

11. **DEFAULT AND ATTORNEY'S FEES.** If Seller executes this agreement, and title to said premises is marketable and insurable and the Buyer neglects or refuses to comply with the terms or any conditions of sale within five (5) days from the date on which said term or condition is to be complied with, then the Earnest Money shall be forfeited and considered as liquidated damages to Seller, and Buyer's interest in the premises shall be immediately terminated. The broker shall pay from said Earnest Money the costs of title insurance, escrow fees, attorney fees and any other expenses directly incurred in connection with this transaction and the remainder shall be apportioned one-half to the Seller and one-half to the broker, provided the amount to broker does not exceed the agreed commission. Such forfeiture and acceptance by Seller and broker of the Earnest Money as liquidated damages does not constitute a waiver of other remedies available to Seller and broker.

In the event of default by either of the parties in their performance of the terms and conditions of this agreement, the defaulting party agrees to pay all attorney fees and costs incurred by the non-defaulting party.

In the event of a dispute between the parties as to the Earnest Money deposited hereunder by Buyer, the Broker, holding the Earnest Money deposit may file an interpleader action in a court of competent jurisdiction to resolve any such dispute between the parties. The Buyer and the Seller authorize the Broker holding the Earnest Money deposit to utilize as much of the Earnest Money deposit as may be necessary to advance the costs and fees required for filing of any such action.

12. **INCLUDED ITEMS.** All attached floor coverings, attached television antenna, attached plumbing, bathroom and lighting fixtures, window screens, screen doors, storm windows, storm doors, window coverings, exterior trees, plants, or shrubbery, water heating apparatus and fixtures, attached fireplace equipment, awnings, ventilating, cooling and heating systems, built in and "drop in" ranges (but excepting all other ranges), fuel tanks and irrigation fixtures and equipment, and any and all, if any, water and water rights, and any and all, if any, ditches and ditch rights that are appurtenant thereto that are now on or used in connection with the premises shall be included in the sale unless otherwise provided herein.

13. **FINANCING REQUIREMENTS.** If financing is required, the Buyer agrees to make a best effort to procure same and further agrees to make application therefore within three (3) banking days after Seller's acceptance of this agreement. If VA or FHA financing is contemplated, additional provisions pertaining thereto may be attached thereto and are thereby incorporated herein by reference.

14. **FHA/VA.** If this agreement is contingent upon Buyer obtaining FHA or VA financing, Buyer and Seller agree that, notwithstanding any other provisions of this contract, Buyer shall not be obligated to complete the purchase of the property described herein **unless** Buyer has received a written statement issued by the FHA or VA as applicable setting forth an appraised value of the property (excluding closing costs) equal to or greater than the purchase price herein. The Buyer may, nevertheless, at his sole discretion proceed under the terms of this agreement provided he shall agree to pay in cash the difference between the asking price stated herein and the appraised value. Buyer shall in either circumstance be obligated to pay normal closing costs attributable to Buyer including but not limited to credit report fees and other loan charges. **The appraised valuation is arrived at to determine the maximum mortgage the Department of Housing and Urban Development will insure. HUD does not warrant the value or the condition of the property. The purchaser should satisfy himself/herself that the price and the condition of the property are acceptable.**

It is agreed that any item included in Paragraph #4 is of nominal value less than $100.

Seller understands that in order for a Buyer to finance through FHA, VA or a conventional lender, those agencies may require that the property comply with the housing code and other governmental requirements of the city or county in which it is located, and may require other inspections. Seller authorizes the selling agent herein to request a City Code Compliance inspection. Seller agrees to pay, in advance, upon request of agent, costs of any of the above inspections.

15. **CONTINGENCY CLAUSE.** If Buyer's offer is contingent upon certain specified conditions occurring, as specified in Item #3 of this agreement, Seller shall have the right to continue to offer the herein property for sale and to accept offers until such time as said contingencies have been satisfied or waived by Buyer. Should Seller receive another acceptable offer to purchase, Seller shall give Buyer three banking days written notice of such offer. In the event Buyer does not waive or satisfy the contingencies in writing within the three-day period, then this Agreement shall be terminated and all deposits returned to Buyer less customary Buyer's costs. In the event Buyer does waive or satisfy the contingencies then Buyer shall proceed to purchase the property under the remaining terms and conditions of this Agreement notwithstanding that the terms of the new offer may be more or less favorable. Notice shall be considered given and the three days shall commence on the earlier of either personal delivery of notice to the Buyer or his agent or two days following the date of mailing evidenced by the postmark on the envelope containing such notice. Notice shall expire at midnight on the third banking day after notice. All notices shall be sent to the addresses shown on the front page of this agreement.

NOTE: Any waiver by the Buyer under this section will be a waiver of ALL contingencies, including financing.

16. **TITLE INSURANCE.** The Seller shall within a reasonable time after closing furnish to the Buyer a title insurance policy in the amount of the purchase price of the premises showing marketable and insurable title subject to the liens, encumbrances and defects elsewhere set out in this agreement to be discharged or assumed by the Buyer. Prior to closing the transaction, the Seller shall furnish to the Buyer a commitment for a title insurance policy showing the condition of the title to said premises. Buyer shall have five (5) days from receipt of the commitment or until 24 hours prior to closing, whichever is the less, within which to object in writing to the condition of the title as set forth in the report. If the Buyer does not so object, the Buyer shall be deemed to have accepted the conditions of the title. It is agreed that if the title of said premises is not marketable, or cannot be made so within thirty (30) days after notice containing a written statement of defects is delivered to the Seller, or if the Seller, having approved said sale fails to consummate the same as herein agreed, the earnest money shall be returned to the Buyer and Seller shall pay for the cost of title insurance, escrow and legal fees, if any.

17. **EXTENDED COVERAGE TITLE POLICY.** A standard policy of title insurance does not cover certain potential problems or risks such as liens (i.e., a legal claim against property for payment of some debt or obligation), boundary disputes, claims of easement, and other matters or claims if they are not of **public record** at time of closing. However, under Idaho law, such potential claims against the property may have become legal obligation **before** the purchase of the home and yet may **not** be of public record until after the purchase. For example, Idaho law allows workmen who have built a new home or remodeled an existing one to file liens against that property for a period of time after they last worked on the home. The debt in such cases will become a lien or claim against the property itself and, if not paid by the Seller, must be paid by the Buyer to protect the equity in the home. Title insurance companies may be able to issue an "extended coverage" policy for an additional premium. In addition to the premium for extended coverage title policy, there may be other costs involved (i.e., survey, additional closing fees). Such a policy **may** protect the Buyer against problems such as the above. Of course, even an "extended coverage" policy contains exclusions and will not insure against all potential problems or risks involved in buying property. It is recommended that the Buyer talk to a title insurance company about what it offers in the way of extended coverage. Only the policy itself can tell exactly what type of coverage is offered, so contact a title insurance company for particulars.

18. **TITLE CONVEYANCE.** Title of Seller is to be conveyed by warranty deed, unless otherwise provided, and is to be marketable and insurable except for rights reserved in federal patents, state or railroad deeds, building or use restrictions, building and zoning regulations and ordinances of any governmental unit, and rights of way and easements established or of record. Liens, encumbrances or defects to be discharged by Seller may be paid out of purchase money at date of closing. No liens, encumbrances or defects, which are to be discharged or assumed by Buyer or to which title is taken subject to, exists unless otherwise specified herein on the front page of this agreement under OTHER FINANCING, TERMS & CONDITIONS.

19. **RISK OF LOSS.** Prior to closing of this sale, all risk of loss shall remain with the Seller. In addition, should the premises be materially damaged by fire or other cause prior to closing, this agreement shall be voidable at the option of the Buyer.

20. **INSPECTION.** The Buyer hereby acknowledges further that he has not received or relied upon any statements or representation by the broker or his representatives or by the Seller which are not herein expressed. The Buyer has entered into this agreement relying solely upon information and knowledge obtained from his own investigation or personal inspection of the premises. This agreement constitutes the whole agreement between the parties and no warranties, including any warranty of habitability, agreements or representations have been made or shall be binding upon either party unless herein set forth.

Each of the parties acknowledges reading and understanding this agreement in full.

Buyer's initial _____   Seller's initial _____

STATE OF IDAHO   )
                                                  : ss
)
County of _____
On this _____ day of _____ 19 _____, before me, the undersigned, a Notary Public in and for said state, personally appeared _____,
known to me to be the person(s) who signed the foregoing instrument as Seller and acknowledged to me that _____ he _____ executed the same. IN WITNESS WHEREOF, I have hereunto set my hand and affixed my seal the day and year first above written.

Notary Public for Idaho _____ Residing at _____

QUESTIONS

1. Shirley U. Jest wants to know the value of her home. Shirley offers to pay Harvey, her neighbor and a qualified appraiser, $200 to appraise her residence. Harvey produces an appraisal three days later. The agreement between Harvey and Shirley U. Jest was:

   a. implied.
   b. bilateral.
   c. unilateral.
   d. executed.

2. When a contract appears to be good and binding but in fact one of the parties may legally reject it, the contract is said to be:

   a. unenforceable.
   b. valid.
   c. void.
   d. voidable.

3. Broker Albert Gordon contracted with Sam and Judith Durrell to sell a parcel of land that the Durrells owned. Gordon was to be paid a specified commission and the parties signed a written agreement. Gordon did find a buyer who made an offer that the Durrells accepted and the sale was completed, but Gordon never received his commission. If Gordon wishes to institute legal proceedings to force the Durrells to pay his commission as provided in the contract, he must do so within:

   a. seven years after payment is due.
   b. six years after payment is due.
   c. five years after payment is due.
   d. four years after payment is due.

4. According to Idaho law, which of the following persons, has the legal capacity to enter into a real estate contract?

   a. An exceptional psychiatric patient, legally declared to be of unsound mind, who obtains written authorization from the attending physician
   b. A registered "foreign" corporation?
   c. A criminal currently imprisoned for automobile theft, who receives permission from the warden of that penal institution
   d. A married 17-year-old

5. Homeowner Alice Potter put a For Sale sign in front of her house. The DeYoungs, after inspecting the property, offer to purchase it for $40,000. Potter accepts; however, the agreement is never expressed in a written contract. Should the DeYoungs fail to perform the agreement and purchase the property, Potter:

   a. cannot take legal action to force the DeYoungs to purchase the house as promised.
   b. may sue the DeYoungs for damages.
   c. may sue the DeYoungs for specific performance.
   d. may sue the DeYoungs for partial performance.

6. Which of the following items need *not* be included in a purchase and sale agreement?

   a. A list of fixtures attached to the property that specifies which of them will be included in the sale and which will not be included
   b. A physical description of the land and improvements, including the type of construction, the number of rooms and their dimensions and the type of heating equipment
   c. A legal description of the location and boundaries of the property given in enough detail so that the exact property can be identified from the description
   d. A list of any personal property that will be included in the sale

7. Which of the following general statements is true regarding the earnest money provision?

   a. The contract must provide for a disposition of the earnest money if the buyer does not complete the sale.
   b. The contract should state only the sales price, leaving the details of how the buyer will pay for the property to be settled at the closing.
   c. The seller promises to furnish the buyer with evidence that he or she owns the property. Any liens or encumbrances that will remain outstanding against the property will be detailed in the title evidence and need not be listed in the earnest money agreement.
   d. After the buyer has signed the agreement and thus made an offer, the seller has an unlimited amount of time in which to reject it or accept and sign the agreement.

8. Which of the following is *not* included in a broker's responsibilities regarding the earnest money provision he or she has negotiated?

    a. Giving a copy of the agreement to the buyer after he or she signs it as a receipt for the earnest money accepted by the broker
    b. Conveying the written offer promptly to the seller and then, after the seller accepts, giving a true copy of the executed agreement to both buyer and seller
    c. Obtaining both parties' written approval for any changes or alterations in the contract
    d. Suggesting that both buyer and seller engage an attorney to explain all the terms and conditions of the contract to them

9. Richard Cleary has signed a purchase and sale agreement to purchase a parcel of real estate for $50,000; however, Cleary must borrow $45,000 (or 90 percent of the purchase price) in order to complete the sale. The lender to whom Cleary will apply for financing has a policy of never lending a real estate purchaser a sum that is greater than 80 percent of the purchase price. Cleary asks the broker to draw a second purchase and sale agreement stating that he will purchase the property for $60,000. He plans to present this second contract to the lender when he applies to borrow $45,000. This kind of practice is:

    a. known as novation.
    b. standard procedure in many Idaho localities.
    c. prohibited by the Idaho Real Estate Commission Rules and Regulations.
    d. permitted provided that the broker obtains the seller's written consent before completing the second contract form.

10. An earnest money deposit received by a broker immediately must be:

    a. placed in the broker's office safe where it must remain until the transaction is closed.
    b. deposited in a special trust bank account maintained by the broker for this purpose or with a neutral escrow depository.
    c. delivered to the seller to whom it belongs.
    d. attached to the broker's copy of the earnest money agreement and retained in the broker's files until the transaction is closed.

11

Transfer of Title

DESCENT AND DISTRIBUTION

Idaho has adopted a modified version of the Uniform Probate Code, which provides for the ownership succession of real property owned by a person who died intestate (without leaving a valid will). The deceased's surviving spouse and issue are always heirs. Other heirs are detailed in the following sections of the law. This pattern of succession does not apply to real estate that the decedent owned as a joint tenant or a tenant by the entirety.

One-half of the community property is owned by the surviving spouse who receives, in addition thereto, property and estate enumerated in Idaho Code Section 15-2-102, as follows:

15-2-102. Share of the spouse—The intestate share of the surviving spouse is as follows:
    (a) *As to separate property*:
    (1) if there is no surviving issue or parent of the decedent, the entire intestate estate;
    (2) if there is no surviving issue but the decedent is survived by a parent or parents, the first fifty thousand dollars ($50,000), plus one-half (1/2) of the balance of the intestate estate;
    (3) if there are surviving issue all of whom are issue of the surviving spouse also, the first fifty thousand dollars ($50,000), plus one-half (1/2) of the balance of the intestate estate;
    (4) if there are surviving issue one (1) or more of whom are not the issue of the surviving spouse, one-half (1/2) of the intestate estate.
    (b) *As to community property*:
    (1) the one-half (1/2 of community property that belongs to the decedent passes to the surviving spouse [I.C. , #15-2-102, as added by 1971, ch. 111, #1, p. 233].

15-2-103. Share of heirs other than surviving spouse—The part of the intestate estate not passing to the surviving spouse under Section 15-2-102 of this part, or the entire intestate estate if there is no surviving spouse, passes as follows:
    (a) to the issue of the decedent; if they are all of the same degree, then those of more remote degree take by representation;
    (b) if there is no surviving issue, to his or her parent or parents equally;
    (c) if there is no surviving issue or parent, to the issue of the parents or either of them by representation;
    (d) if there is no surviving issue, parent or issue of a parent, but the decedent is survived by one (1) or more grandparents or issue of grandparents, half of the estate passes to the paternal grandparents if both survive, or to the surviving paternal grandparent, or to the issue of the paternal grandparents if both are deceased, the issue taking equally if they are all of the same degree of kinship to the decedent, but if of unequal degree those of more remote degree take by representation; and the other half passes to the maternal relatives in the same manner; but if there be no surviving grandparent or issue of grandparents on either the paternal or the maternal side, the entire estate passes to the relatives on the other side in the

same manner as the half [I.C., #15-2-103, as added by 1971, ch. 111, # 1, p. 233; am. 1973, ch. 167, #5, p. 319].

15-1-201 (25). "Issue" of a person means all his or her lineal descendants of all generations, with the relationship of parent and child at each generation being determined by the definitions of child and parent contained in this code.

If no heirs are found, the entire intestate estate passes to the state of Idaho, subject to administration by the public administrator. The estate is then disposed of under the Unclaimed Property Act, and if not claimed within 1,827 days from the date the property is paid to the State Tax Commission, it escheats to the state and is apportioned to the public school fund.

TRANSFER OF TITLE BY WILL

This method of transferring a decedent's real estate is described in the text. A will must be prepared and executed by the property owner during his or her lifetime but cannot take effect until after the property owner's death. In Idaho any emancipated minor or any person 18 or more years of age who is sound of mind may make a will.

Every will (with certain limited exceptions) must be in writing and signed by the testator or in the testator's name by some other person in the testator's presence and by his or her direction. It also must be signed by at least two persons, each of whom witnessed either the signing of the will or the testator's acknowledgment of the signature or of the will. A *holographic will* is one in which the material provisions of the will and the signature are in the handwriting of the testator. There need be no witnesses to a holographic will. A *nuncupative will* is a verbal will made under special circumstances in immediate anticipation of the maker's death; however, the Idaho Uniform Probate Code has no provision for the use or enforceability of this type of will.

TRANSFER OF TITLE BY INVOLUNTARY ACTION OF LAW

Involuntary transfer comes in many forms. *Accession* is a growth or increase of real property, frequently involving riparian or littoral (shoreline) property. Such land may be increased by *accretion*, which means through natural forces. Accretion may be accomplished by the process of *alluvion*, in which soil is washed up on the banks and deposited gradually, or by *reliction*, in which the water recedes permanently and lowers the waterline. Accession also may include improvements made by others to an owner's land or buildings that cannot be removed and so become *fixtures*.

Transfer by *adverse possession* is described in the text. A person who claims to acquire title to a parcel of real estate by adverse possession in Idaho must have been adversely in possession for *five years*. Such a person also *must have paid all taxes legally assessed against the property during this period*. The similar acquisition of an easement by prescription is discussed in Chapter 7 of the text and this Supplement.

Bankruptcy is a legal proceeding created to protect the rights of debtors and their creditors when an insolvent person is unable to repay debts. Bankruptcy may be either voluntary or involuntary and takes the form, for most individuals and businesses, of a Chapter 7, a Chapter 11 or a Chapter 13. A *Chapter 7* is total insolvency. The court appoints a "trustee" who takes control of the bankrupt's nonexempt assets and liquidates them to repay the creditors. A *Chapter 11* is available to individuals in business or businesses and is a form of reorganization that usually allows the bankrupt to dispose of assets in such a manner as to suffer the least amount of asset devaluation due to a forced sale. Also there must be, in the opinion of the court, enough assets available to satisfy the creditors. The court appoints a "trustee," who may be the bankrupt. (Such debtor is called a "debtor in possession.") The trustee then takes control and title of the bankrupt person's nonexempt assets; those assets are sold with court approval, and the funds are applied toward the bankrupt's debts and other provable claims. A *Chapter 13* is often called a "wage-earner plan" and allows the bankrupt to file a plan, which is approved by the court, for repayment of debts to all the creditors.

Eminent domain is discussed in the text., Escheat is described in the text and in this chapter in the section entitled "Descent and Distribution."

Confiscation

Confiscation is the taking of property by a government in time of emergency or war without paying compensation. Generally only property of enemies of the government is confiscated. Private property also has been confiscated when someone profits from an illegal act.

GIFTS

Title to real property may be transferred voluntarily by gift or sale. Gifts of real estate may involve transfers to private persons, or to municipal governments by *dedication*. Land for streets, alleys, parks and other public uses may be dedicated for public use by one of two methods.

Statutory dedication involves a recorded subdivision plat that indicates that specific streets or areas are set aside for public use. Such a plat must include a certificate executed by all parties who have a recorded interest in the property and are offering the specified areas for dedication as well as a certificate of acceptance executed by the proper municipal officials. *Common law dedication* includes all other less-formal dedications, for example, when a property owner clearly indicates in some way that a certain portion of his or her land is intended for public use. Acceptance of such a common law dedication may be by actual public use of the property or by a resolution of the city council. A common law dedication is considered to convey an *easement* to the public, with the landowner retaining the fee title to the property.

DEEDS

The execution and delivery of a deed is the method provided by law for landowners to convey, transfer or release their interests in real estate while they are living. After a deed has been executed and delivered, the grantor's interest in the property is transferred subject to the legal rights and covenants that the law attaches to the kind and form of deed used. A deed may be delivered only once. The text describes various forms of deeds and the requirements for a valid deed of conveyance. The following additional information is important to an understanding of the deeds used in Idaho.

Forms of Deeds

The most common form of deed used in Idaho is the *warranty deed*, which incorporates the grant deed. A *grant deed* is a statutory form of deed in which the word *grant* implies that the grantor and his or her heirs are bound by the following covenants and no others:

1. The grantor previously has not conveyed the same estate or any part of it to any person other than the grantee.

2. The estate conveyed is free from encumbrances done, made or suffered by the grantor or any person claiming under the grantor.

In warranty deeds and bargain and sale deeds that customarily use the words *grant* or *grant, bargain and sell* as words of conveyance, the covenants by which the grantor is bound are written out. Such covenants may grant full warranty or they may grant special warranty, which covers only the grantor's acts during the ownership period.

Grant deeds, warranty deeds and bargain and sale deeds are generally interpreted by Idaho law as passing *after-acquired title*. For example, a grantor actually had less of an interest in the property at the time of conveyance than supposed, or a defective interest. If after the conveyance, the grantor acquired title or perfected the title, such after-acquired title would automatically pass to the grantee.

By using a quitclaim deed, the grantor releases whatever interest in the property he or she may have, if any, to the grantee. No warranties or covenants are implied or written in this type of deed. It transfers only such title, right or interest in the property that the grantor had at the time the quitclaim is delivered. After-acquired title does not pass under a quitclaim deed unless specifically provided for on the face of the deed.

A deed conveying real estate as a gift may state that "love and affection" is the consideration given for the property; this is known as a *gift deed*.

In Chapter 14/15 of the text and this Supplement, a *release deed* is described as conveying or releasing the title or interest of a trust deed under a deed of trust loan after the debt has been paid in full by the landowner borrower. In Idaho this special type of deed is referred to as a *reconveyance deed*.

Acknowledgment

Acknowledgment, as described in the text, enables deeds and other instruments to be recorded. In Idaho acknowledgments may be taken by notary publics, county recorders, clerks, judges of courts of record and certain other public officials. Any acknowledgment is void if it is taken by a notary or other authorized person who is also a party to the transaction. Idaho statutes provide for the specific wording of the acknowledgment depending on the capacity of the signatory (i.e., attorney-in-fact, corporate officer, etc.).

Revenue Stamps

Idaho has no documentary stamp tax, transfer fee or other tax on real estate conveyances.

QUESTIONS

1. Phil Raynor is survived by his wife Rhonda and their two daughters. Phil and Rhonda's community property is worth $50,000, but Phil also has left a separate estate worth $150,000. Because Phil died suddenly without leaving a will:

   a. Rhonda acquires sole ownership of the community property and her daughters each receive $75,000 from Phil's separate property.
   b. Rhonda acquires sole ownership of all of the property.
   c. Rhonda receives $50,000 (all of the community property) and $100,000 from Phil's separate property, and her daughters each receive $25,000.
   d. Rhonda receives one-half of the entire estate, or $25,000 from the community property and $75,000 from Phil's separate property, whereas her daughters each receive one-half of the balance of the entire estate, or $50,000.

2. Emily McMillan died intestate leaving an estate worth $30,000. Because Emily had no family, after five years her property passed into the state public school fund through the principle of:

   a. accession.
   b. escheat.
   c. eminent domain.
   d. dedication.

3. Shortly before his death Edgar Hodges wrote out his will, signed it and placed it on his desk for his family to find. This type of will is known as a:

   a. holographic will.
   b. nuncupative will.
   c. probate will.
   d. formal will.

4. Joseph Kramer's property lies on the bank of a small river. Over the years the river has flowed past Kramer's property, depositing soil along the bank. This gradual increase of Kramer's lands is known as:

   a. littoral distribution.
   b. dereliction.
   c. escheat.
   d. alluvion.

5. A businessman inherited an old farmhouse from his aunt but was too busy to inspect the property immediately. A young couple in need of a place to live found the empty farmhouse and moved in. Six months later there still was no sign of the absent owner and the couple began to make repairs on the property. In order to acquire ownership of this property by adverse possession the couple must:

   a. occupy and use the property in this way continuously, for a period of five years.
   b. after using the property continuously for five years, locate the businessman and pay him a token consideration for title to the property.
   c. occupy and use the property continuously for five years, paying all real estate taxes and assessments for the property during this time.
   d. file a declaration of homestead in the county record and occupy and use the property for five years.

6. George Dubois sold his home and delivered a warranty deed to the new owners. One month later Dubois was informed that a third party, Joan West, had a claim to the property arising from an improperly executed deed to a former owner. To correct this situation West executed a quitclaim deed to Dubois conveying her interest in the property. This perfected interest, which passed to the new owner, is known as:

   a. accession.
   b. quitclaim title.
   c. after-acquired title.
   d. involuntary alienation.

7. A grant deed:

   a. warrants that the grantor previously has not conveyed or encumbered the real estate.
   b. conveys any interest the grantor may have in the real estate.
   c. usually lists love and affection as the consideration given in exchange for the real estate.
   d. is subject to the Idaho realty transfer tax.

8. Which of the following is *not* an example of transfer of title by involuntary action of law?

   a. Accretion
   b. Confiscation
   c. Bankruptcy
   d. Eminent domain

12

Title Records

RECORDING DOCUMENTS

Any conveyance, instrument or judgment affecting title to or possession of real estate may be recorded. An instrument must be acknowledged, or proven and certified, in order to be eligible for recording. Then it is deposited in the Recorder's Office of the county in which the property is located and the proper fee is paid. (*Note*: Deeds must contain the grantee's correct mailing address.)

The courts charge the prospective buyer of real estate with constructive notice, making him or her responsible for knowing what documents are in the public record concerning the property. Documents are filed and indexed in the public record according to the grantor's and grantee's names and according to the legal description of the property involved. Recorded documents give constructive notice from the time they are filed with the county recorder. Recording also establishes the priority of rights. A deed or other interest in real property that is recorded outside the chain of title may not be located by an individual going to the recorder's office because the recorder, using a grantor/grantee index, lists any and all documents recorded in either name. and if these names are not known, the recorded document could not be found.

Unrecorded documents, including deeds, are valid between the parties to the transaction; however, they do not protect the rights of such parties against subsequent purchasers or lenders who do not have actual notice of them and cannot learn of them by inspecting the public record.

Foreign Language Documents

Idaho law makes no special provision for documents written in a foreign language. The recorder will accept for recording any document that is properly acknowledged and notarized.

UNRECORDED INTERESTS

Constructive notice, as described in the text, charges the buyer of real estate with the responsibility of inspecting the property as well as searching the public record. A person claiming an interest in a parcel of real estate can give notice of his or her right by being in possession of the property. For example, a purchaser who has not recorded the deed may take possession and thus give notice of the interest. (This is not to suggest that a purchaser need not record the deed; all deeds should be recorded promptly.) An inspection of the property will reveal who is in possession and other possible unrecorded interests, such as an easement that is in actual use, a neighbor's fence or wall encroaching on the property or evidence of recent construction work indicating the possibility of as yet unrecorded mechanics' liens against the property. This type of constructive notice is referred to as "inquiry notice."

TITLE EVIDENCE

In most Idaho real estate sales transactions, the seller is required to furnish evidence of his or her good title to the property being sold. In Idaho the title abstract, as described in the text, is acceptable evidence of title. This history of recorded documents affecting the title to a parcel of real estate must be examined and evaluated by a real estate attorney, who then prepares an opinion of the title or ownership rights.

The protection afforded by a title company is that it cross-indexes all the documents recorded in a given county against a plat. Asking for a preliminary title report or title information ensures that all transfers outside the chain of title have been picked up by someone who has been keeping record on a day-to-day basis on a plat index and not just by a grantor-grantee index.

The Idaho Real Estate Commission's Rules and Regulations expressly forbids real estate licensees from passing judgment or giving opinions on the merchantability or condition of the title to a parcel of real property. This is a task for an attorney and the licensee must not discourage either party to the transaction from consulting an attorney in such matters.

Title Insurance

In Idaho the title insurance industry is closely regulated by the Department of Insurance as to rates charged, rebates of fees, kinds of free services allowed and gifts that may be offered to the title insurance clients.

Abstracts of title are now seldom used in Idaho because of the preferable protection offered by title insurance policies. Title insurance protects against suits or claims based on items that are insured in the policy. The title company will defend any such suits at its own expense. Several forms of title policies are issued; these have been standardized by the American Land Title Association and are known as ALTA forms.

The owner's policy insures the owner's title. The condition of the title is insured as of the date of the policy. As with most title policies, it insures against such problems as forged documents, improperly delivered deeds and documents executed by incompetent parties. It does not insure against those items that are listed as exceptions, including the following: defects in the title known to the owner; unrecorded easements; mechanics' liens and other liens, claims or rights; rights of parties in possession not indicated in the public record; encroachments; factors that would be disclosed by an accurate survey and inspection of the property; and governmental regulations, such as zoning requirements, building codes or eminent domain.

The mortgage or loan policy (lender's policy) provides coverage that is not usually included in the owner's policy. It insures the condition of the mortgage or deed of trust loan for the lender. All liens against the property are determined to evaluate the priority of the mortgage lien. This policy insures only the lender, not the owner. In a sale where the buyer is financing the purchase with a mortgage or deed of trust loan, however, both the owner's and lender's policies can be ordered together and prepared from the same title search.

Extended coverage. Extended coverage beyond what is provided in a standard lender's policy is now available to a lender and also to an owner, purchaser or lessee. This coverage insures against rights of persons who are in possession of the property; certain mechanics' liens; validity of the lender's lien (except for usury or violation of truth-in-lending laws); lien priority; and street assessments.

Before an extended coverage policy is issued, the premises must be inspected by the title insurance agent and investigations must be made for possible off-record defects, liens or encumbrances. The title company charges additional fees for the extended coverage and possibly for the inspection. In some cases, a survey is required.

Torrens System

The Torrens system of registering title to real estate has not been adopted in Idaho.

BUSINESS OPPORTUNITY SALES

Every business, no matter how small, must have a place of operation. Whether it is a small direct-mail sales enterprise operated from the owner's home, or a large manufacturing concern with numerous factories and sales offices, the operation of a business involves the use of real estate. Consequently, when a business is sold, the title or lease to real estate used in the business is usually included in the sale. For this reason, a *person who sells or negotiates the sale of businesses for others for a fee is required to be licensed as a real estate broker*.

Chapter 10 of the text and this Supplement detailed what must be included in a valid real estate sales contract (earnest money agreement or receipt and agreement to purchase). When the sale includes chattel (trade fixtures) and other items of personal property as well as an interest in real estate, an additional agreement must be executed by the seller. Items of personal property may be listed in the real estate sales contract. They should not, however, be included in a deed granting title to real property. At the closing of a business sales transaction, a separate *bill of sale* should be executed by the seller for all chattel, stock, materials and other items of personal property that are included in the sale.

Uniform Commercial Code

The Uniform Commercial Code, as described in the text, was adopted in Idaho in 1967 with some variations and alternate provisions. The section of the code that is most applicable to the real estate business is Article 6, which covers bulk transfers. A general discussion of the Code and Article 6 is included in the text.

In most businesses, supplies, goods and services constantly are being purchased on credit and paid for periodically as the suppliers submit their bills. The regulations involving bulk transfers are designed to protect the creditors of a business from the fraud that may be perpetrated by a business owner who sells the business, including equipment and stock, then disappears leaving creditors unpaid. In such a case, the creditors cannot follow the conveyed goods and demand payment from the new owner unless it can be proved that the new owner had actual knowledge of the fraud.

To prevent such a fraud from occurring in the sale of a business, the purchaser should require the seller to execute a *bulk sales affidavit*. This is a sworn statement listing any liens or unpaid bills that might become liens against the stock, fixtures or furniture included in the sale. A list of creditors should be included, specifying the amount due to each creditor. In addition, the purchaser must notify each creditor of the pending sale by registered mail, at least five days before the sale takes place. The purchaser of a business who fails to obtain a bulk sales affidavit from the seller or fails to give creditors due notice can be held responsible for unpaid invoices, even though he or she paid the seller in good faith for the full value of the items involved.

QUESTIONS

1. An instrument affecting the title to a parcel of real estate gives constructive notice to the world when it is filed with the:

   a. city clerk.
   b. county recorder.
   c. Idaho Real Estate Commission.
   d. title company.

2. To be eligible for recording in Idaho, a document must be:

   a. in English.
   b. witnessed by two persons who are not affected by the document.
   c. acknowledged.
   d. drawn up by an attorney.

3. John Vacarro is interested in purchasing a certain large parcel of real estate from Edward Draper. Draper does not live on the property. Which of the following facts about the property could Vacarro *not* discover by inspecting it?

   a. A family is, without Draper's knowledge, living in an abandoned house on the property.
   b. The local bank holds a mortgage loan against the property.
   c. The local telephone company has an easement across the property where telephone poles and wires are installed.
   d. A fence, erected by the nearest neighbor to the east of the property, actually stands on Draper's land, two feet west of the property line.

4. In most real estate sales transactions that take place in Idaho, the seller is required to present as evidence of good title to the property being sold a(n):

   a. abstract of title with an attorney's opinion.
   b. Torrens certificate.
   c. attorney's certificate of title.
   d. title insurance policy.

5. Carl and Nancy Hayworth are purchasing a small hardware firm from Ralph Busch, who is planning to retire. Busch will be moving to Arizona after the sale is finalized and the Hayworths do not want to be held liable for any debts he may have incurred in connection with the business. The Uniform Commercial Code provides that the Hayworths can protect themselves by:

   a. obtaining a list of Busch's creditors from the local credit bureau and including a provision in the sales contract that such creditors must be paid before the sale can be closed.
   b. having Busch issue a sworn statement at the closing that the Hayworths are not liable for any such debts.
   c. obtaining Busch's new address so that any such claims by creditors can be referred directly to him.
   d. requiring Busch to execute a sworn statement listing all of his creditors and the amounts owed to each, and then informing each creditor of the sale by registered mail at least five days before it is scheduled to take place.

6. Idaho title companies are controlled by the:

    a. Real Estate Commission.
    b. American Land Title Association.
    c. Insurance Commission.
    d. county board of commissioners.

13

Real Estate License Law

NOTICE: IT IS IMPORTANT THAT YOU UNDERSTAND THAT THE INFORMATION IN THIS SEC-TION IS A SUMMARY OF THE IDAHO REAL ESTATE LICENSE LAW. YOU MUST CHECK THE CURRENT COPY OF THE IDAHO LICENSE LAW AND RULES AND REGULATIONS FOR THE LAT-EST CHANGES AND UPDATES THAT MAY HAVE BEEN ADOPTED SINCE THIS TEXTBOOK WAS LAST PRINTED AND/OR REVISED.

REAL ESTATE LICENSE LAW

The Idaho Real Estate License Law, Chapter 20, Title 54 of the Idaho Code, was first enacted in 1947 and amended in 1951, 1969, 1970, 1971, 1974, 1975, 1976, 1978, 1980, 1981, 1982, 1983, 1985, 1987, 1988 and 1989. (No amendments were made in 1984, 1986 or 1990.) The Idaho Real Estate Commission regulates real estate activity in the state. You can obtain a current copy of this law by writing to the Idaho Real Estate Commission, Statehouse Mail, Boise, Idaho 83720.

The license law is divided into two parts. In addition to the law itself, the commission, as authorized by the law, has adopted a number of rules and regulations that elaborate on the basic law and provide additional guidelines for Idaho real estate licensees. The summaries of the law and the Rules and Regulations of the Idaho Real Estate Commission presented in this chapter are intended to acquaint you with their general provisions. The Rules and Regulations *require* Idaho licensees to know the Idaho Real Estate License Law and Rules and Regulations.

WHO MUST BE LICENSED

According to Section 54-2021, no person can engage in the real estate business or act as a real estate broker or salesperson in Idaho without first obtaining a license. The penalty for a person convicted of op-erating without a license is a fine of up to $1,000 and/or imprisonment for up to one year. The penalty for corporations is a fine of up to $2,500 (Section 54-2044). In addition, no person engaged in the real estate business or acting as a broker or salesperson may file a court suit to collect payment for such activ-ities unless that person can prove that he or she was properly licensed at the time the activities or services in question were performed (Section 54-2045).

Definitions

Real estate broker (Section 54-2022). A *real estate broker* is defined as any person who, while acting for another person for compensation or the promise of compensation, performs any of the following activities with regard to real estate, business opportunities or an interest in either:

1. sells,

2. lists,

3. buys,

4. directly or indirectly negotiates the purchase, sale or exchange of real estate or a business opportunity,

5. offers to perform or negotiate one of these transactions,

6. represents or advertises to the public in any way that he or she engages in any of these activities,

7. takes part in any way in procuring prospects or in negotiating or closing any transaction that is intended to result in one of these activities, and

8. buys, sells or offers to buy or sell options, or otherwise acts as a dealer in options.

Associate real estate broker. Section 54-2022 also defines an *associate broker* as any person who qualifies as a real estate broker, is licensed under and associated with a designated broker and who directly or indirectly represents that broker in the performance of any of the activities described under the definition of broker. The associate broker's license names the specific broker with whom he or she is associated.

Real estate salesman. In addition Section 54-2022 defines a real estate *salesman* (salesperson) as any person who is licensed under and associated with a designated broker and who directly or indirectly represents that broker in the performance of any of the previously described activities.

Person. The word *person*, as used throughout the license law and defined in Section 54-2023, refers to an individual, partnership or corporation.

Business opportunity. The term *business opportunity* is defined to include an established business, the goodwill of an established business or any interest in a business for which a sale or transfer of an interest in land is involved in the transaction (this includes an assignment of a lease).

Dealer in options. An *option* is a contract conveying a right to buy or sell real estate at a specified price during a stipulated period. Any person, firm, partnership, association or corporation who directly or indirectly takes, obtains or uses options to purchase, exchange, rent, or lease real property for another person is a *dealer in options*. It makes no difference if the options are in the dealer's name or if title to the real estate in question is ever held briefly by the dealer in connection with the ultimate transaction.

Exceptions (Section 54-2024)

The Idaho Real Estate License Law does not apply to the following persons, provided they are not active Idaho real estate licensees:

1. any person who purchases any real estate, option in real property or business opportunity for his or her own use or who sells, exchanges or otherwise disposes of his or her own real estate,

2. any person who holds a property owner's power of attorney when that power of attorney was given for the purpose of completing a single transaction,

3. any owner or any regular, salaried employee of the owner acting within the scope of his or her employment, who sells, exchanges, purchases or carries out any other disposition of property or business opportunity,

4. any attorney at law acting in the performance of his or her regular duties,

5. any receiver, trustee in bankruptcy, guardian, administrator, executor or personal representative of an estate,

6. any person acting under a court order or selling under a deed of trust, and

7. a property management, rental or leasing agent.

THE IDAHO REAL ESTATE COMMISSION (Sections 54-2025 through 54-2027)

Organization and Members

The Idaho Real Estate Commission was created in 1947, as authorized by the license law. The commission is composed of four members: one each from the northern, southeastern, southwestern and south central sections of the state. All are appointed by the governor. The law requires that commission members be licensed real estate brokers with at least five years' experience in the real estate business in Idaho. The members are paid $25 per day plus expenses while working for the commission, as provided by Section 59-509(f) of the Idaho Code.

Each commission member serves a four-year term; the appointments are staggered so that one member's term expires each year. Upon the death, resignation or removal of any member, the governor will appoint a qualified successor to serve out the unexpired term. The governor may remove a member from office for neglect of duty, incompetency or unprofessional or dishonorable behavior.

Duties and Powers

Each year the commission selects one member to serve as chairman. In administering and enforcing the license law, the commission has the power to create and enforce any necessary rules and regulations. Generally, these regulations clarify the broader provisions of the law and describe more specific requirements for applicants and licensees. In addition, the commission is specifically responsible for conducting examinations to determine the competency of real estate license applicants. No license may be issued by the commission unless a majority of the members agree on the applicant's qualifications.

Records and procedures (Section 54-2052). The commission is also responsible for maintaining records and for making these records open to public inspection. However, the commission may refuse to disclose the following documents without court order:

1. real estate broker's and real estate salesperson's examinations,

2. investigative reports and similar materials prepared, obtained or compiled by the commission's staff while investigating possible violations,

3. the criminal records of licensees or applicants for licenses, and

4. reports of audits of brokers' trust accounts.

Executive Director (Rules and Regulations)

The executive director of the commission is an administrator employed by the commission to direct the operation of its activities. In general the executive director operates the commission's office, hires and supervises the staff and maintains records of all commission activities. The director's responsibilities also include preparing and conducting the examinations, issuing licenses, preparing a news bulletin that is sent to all licensees, investigating complaints of license law violations, taking any necessary action against a licensee and correcting violations (subject to the commission's approval). In addition the executive director is responsible for promoting high standards of practice in the real estate industry by organizing and conducting educational programs.

LICENSING PROCEDURE

Applications and Requirements (Section 54-2029)

An application for a real estate license must be made on a form provided by the Idaho Real Estate Commission. Every applicant must meet the following requirements:

1. be at least 18 years of age,

2. furnish proof to the commission that he or she is a high school graduate or holder of an equivalent certificate of educational achievement from any state,

3. not have had a real estate license revoked or renewal refused in any state within two years before applying for a license in Idaho,

4. not have been convicted, fined, placed on probation, received a withheld sentence, or completed a term of imprisonment from any state or federal court for a felony or any crime involving moral turpitude (immoral activities) within five years before applying for a license in Idaho,

5. show proof of the successful completion of appropriate educational requirements, and

6. show proof of passing the license exam within three months prior to the license application date.

In addition to these general requirements, an applicant for the real estate broker's (or associate broker's) license must have actively worked as a real estate salesperson for two years in Idaho within the five years prior to the application date. The commission may, however, reduce or eliminate this requirement based on the applicant's educational background, experience as a real estate broker in another state or experience in related business activities. The broker license applicant is also required to furnish a report, certified by his or her broker, of listings and sales accomplished by the applicant during the last two years of licensure.

Educational requirement. Applicants for a salesperson's license must successfully complete two 45-hour courses, or equivalent study approved by the commission, in basic real estate principles and practices within five years prior to applying for a license.

Applicants for a broker's license must successfully complete, prior to licensing, a minimum of four courses totaling 90 additional classroom hours or equivalent correspondence study in real estate subjects as approved by the commission. Courses may be taken at any university, college, junior college or privately owned real estate school approved by the commission.

All courses must include a final examination and provide a certificate of successful completion that the applicant must furnish to the commission. An applicant who has completed a course not previously approved by the commission may submit a certificate of completion; the commission then will determine if the course meets its requirements.

Examinations (Section 54-2034)

Every applicant for a real estate broker's, associate broker's or salesperson's license must take and successfully pass a written examination. Each applicant should read the information in the *Candidate Guide*, which is available from the Real Estate Commission, before applying to take the examination. This booklet contains the application for the exam, the subject areas covered on the exam, types of questions, exam-taking techniques and other such pertinent examination information.

The broker's and salesperson's examination is generally given once a month in Boise and bimonthly in Pocatello and Coeur d'Alene. The tests are usually given on the fourth Saturday of each month. Any applicant who wishes to be assured of admission to the license examination must have his or her complete and correct application form together with the proper fee on file with the testing service or postmarked by the filing deadline. Admission tickets will be mailed to candidates who have properly submitted complete registration forms and fees. Admission tickets should be received approximately five days prior to the test date. They will specify the test center location and any specific instructions regarding parking, materials to take to the test center and the like. You must bring the admission ticket with you to the test center, or you may not be admitted. Candidates who for any reason fail to report to their designated test center at the specified time will forfeit fees paid.

The testing service will *not* accept cash or credit cards as payment. Only individual checks or money orders, made payable to the testing service, will be honored.

Walk-in candidates are accepted without preregistration as long as they meet all the requirements for examination; bring with them the completed application form, required identification specified in the *Candidate Guide*, any test materials indicated; and pay the additional walk-in fee. Although every effort will be made by the testing service to accommodate all candidates, walk-in candidates cannot be guaranteed admission to the examination.

All applicants are allowed a three and one-half hour continuous testing session administered over a one-day period. A passing score for the national and state portions combined is 70 on the salesperson's examination and 75 on the broker's examination.

An applicant who fails an examination may retake it on a regularly scheduled examination date. There is no limit to the number of times an applicant may retake an examination.

Fees (Subject to Revision)

Every preregistered applicant for a real estate broker's, associate broker's or salesperson's license exam must pay a nonrefundable examination fee of fifty dollars ($50), as set by law. The fee for those applicants who are not preregistered is sixty dollars ($60). An original license fee ($160) is payable to the commission when the license is issued. The original license expires on the last day of the second consecutive birth month following the original license date. Subsequent license terms are based on a two-year period from birth month to birth month of each licensee. A renewal fee and an application must be submitted to renew either an active or inactive license. Active license renewals must also document successful completion of the continuing education requirement. Included in the license fee is a fee of $20, which is deposited into the Real Estate Recovery Account as provided in Idaho Code, Section 54-2035. Licensees who fail to renew their licenses on time and pay the required fees still may renew within one year after the last renewal date, subject to the commission's approval and a fine of $15 for late renewal. Such licenses are suspended from the time they expire until they are renewed, and the licensee may not engage in real estate activities during that period. The renewal fee is the same as that charged for an original license ($160).

The commission also charges the following service fees:

Each preregistered examination retake	$50
Each walk-in examination retake	60
Change of address (each licensee)	10
Each branch office established	20

Licensing Corporations and Partnerships (Sections 54-2028 and 54-2030)

A corporation or partnership may be granted a broker's license provided that it complies with certain requirements. If the applicant is a corporation, a list of the officers and directors and their addresses must be submitted to the commission along with the application. In addition, one of the officers must be named in the application as the corporation's *designated broker*. This person must qualify as a broker and pass the broker's examination, submitting his or her broker's application at the same time as the corporation's application. No additional bond or fee is necessary for the individual's license. Other officers who can qualify also may be licensed as brokers for the corporation. The license issued for a designated broker of a corporation includes the name of the corporation or corporations. If a licensee is the designated broker of more than one corporation, all such corporations must be located at the same business address and affiliated with or subsidiaries of the main corporation.

With a partnership, all the partners' names and addresses must be submitted with the application, and all of the partners who can qualify as real estate brokers may be named in the application to act as such for the firm. The individual broker's applications should be filed at the same time as the partnership's application, with one partner named as the designated broker to be responsible for the agency.

The commission has the authority to investigate firms to determine whether the corporation or partnership actually exists at the time a license or renewal application is submitted. For this purpose, a corporation shall submit a copy of its corporate minutes and bylaws with the license application, showing that the corporation has appointed a designated broker and naming other officers who may apply to be a broker with the firm. In the case of a partnership, a copy of the partnership agreement shall be submitted with the application.

Reciprocal Licensure (Sections 54-2036, 54-2032 and 54-2033A)

Idaho will grant a real estate salesperson's or broker's license to any nonresident salesperson or broker who is licensed in a state that grants the same privilege to Idaho residents. This is called *reciprocity*, and Idaho has reciprocal agreements with several surrounding states. Such nonresident brokers and salespeople will be issued licenses upon completing the requirements set forth in each agreement. The commission office should be contacted for specific requirements and procedures.

Reciprocal brokers licensed in Idaho must maintain an active place of business in the state in which they live. Such brokers may operate a branch office in Idaho only if that branch is managed by a resident Idaho broker, or they may face revocation or suspension of their licenses under Section 54-2040. In addition a nonresident salesperson will be issued a reciprocal license only if he or she is licensed under a nonresident broker who is also licensed in Idaho.

Irrevocable consent (Section 54-2032). Every nonresident applicant must file an irrevocable consent agreement with the commission for filing with the secretary of state. This document states that suits and actions shall be served in duplicate and may be served against the applicant in any county in Idaho in which the plaintiff having a course of action or suit resides. When such a suit is commenced, one copy of the process or pleading is served on the Idaho secretary of state; the other is immediately forwarded by registered mail to the designated business address of the person against whom the process or pleadings are directed. Properly served, the suit and its outcome will be valid and binding upon the nonresident licensee.

Other nonresidents. Any person who resides in a state that does not grant reciprocity to Idaho residents may obtain a license by meeting the normal requirements for licensure, such as:

1.   meet Idaho education requirements,

2.   make proper application and pay the appropriate license fee, and

3.   become associated with an Idaho real estate broker as a salesperson or associate broker or establish a place of business in Idaho as a broker.

REAL ESTATE RECOVERY ACCOUNT (Section 54-2035, A–K)

Idaho's Real Estate Recovery Account was established in 1971. Every licensee pays a portion of the two-year original or renewal license fee toward the account. A balance of $20,000 is maintained in the account to satisfy claims against Idaho real estate licensees.

Recovery from the Account

The maximum claim that may be paid out of the account is $2,000 per licensee per calendar year. The claim must be based on some fraud, misrepresentation or deceit practiced by the licensee in connection with a real estate transaction. An aggrieved party who wishes to collect a claim from the account has the following possible course of action.

The aggrieved party must start by filing a suit against the licensee. After obtaining a final judgment in any court of competent jurisdiction and after all proceedings, including appeals, are concluded, the aggrieved person then may petition the court to direct payment of the judgment out of the account. A copy of the petition must be served on the commission and the court must hold a hearing and act on the petition within 30 days of that service.

At the hearing the petitioner must show that he or she has obtained a proper judgment and complied with all requirements concerning the account. The petitioner also must show that all possible legal steps were taken to collect the judgment from the defendant licensee and that the licensee does not have enough funds or property to satisfy the judgment. In addition, the petitioner must prove that he or she is not the licensee's spouse or a representative of the licensee's spouse.

At any court action requesting money from the fund to satisfy a claim against a licensee, the commission may take steps to defend the licensee and/or review the case. Based on the commission's findings and subject to the court's approval, the commission may be able to reach a compromise on a petitioner's claim.

Waiver of rights. Any aggrieved person who fails to comply with all regulations concerning the Real Estate Recovery Account loses his or her rights to collect from the account.

Automatic Suspension

Whenever the commission is directed by a court to pay out money from the account, the license of the broker, associate broker or salesperson against whom the claim is made is automatically suspended. This person's license will not be reinstated until he or she has repaid the account with the full amount plus interest at the highest rate allowed by law. The repayment of funds does not nullify or modify the effect of any other disciplinary action the commission may take against the licensee.

Subrogation

After the commission has paid a claim from the account to an aggrieved person, the commission is *subrogated to* (acquires by substitution) all rights to the aggrieved person's claim. Any monies, including interest, then recovered by the commission from the suspended defendant licensee should be deposited in the account.

GENERAL OPERATION OF A REAL ESTATE BUSINESS

Place of Business (Section 54-2038)

Every Idaho real estate broker except those brokers licensed by reciprocity must maintain an office in Idaho as a principal place of business. The broker must conduct business only under the name and at the address indicated on his or her license. In that place of business the broker's license must be prominently displayed along with those of all licensees who work there. It is unlawful for a salesperson to use the broker's license and operate a real estate business in the broker's name when the broker has only nominal control of the business affairs. More than one broker, however, can maintain an office at the same address. Under these circumstances, each broker must keep separate records and trust accounts and operate under a separate and distinct business name that clearly identifies each individual broker.

Branch office. When a broker establishes one or more branch offices, a separate license must be obtained for each branch office, which must operate under the same name as the parent office. The broker is responsible for all business transacted in the branch office.

Every branch office licensed to do business in Idaho must be managed by a licensed broker or associate broker or by a licensed salesperson with two years' active experience. The manager must be designated on the application for a branch office when it is filed with the commission. The commission must be notified of any change in the designated manager of a branch office.

When a branch office is closed and real estate business is no longer transacted at that location, the broker must give the commission written notice of the closing, along with the licenses of all people affiliated with that office. The commission then will process the license transfers of each licensee individually.

Change of business name or location. The commission also must be notified of any change in a licensee's business name or address or branch office. Failure to report a change in business name or address is a violation of Section 54-2038 and may result in the cancellation of the license. Inactive licensees have ten days following any change of address or phone number to report the change to the commission.

Licenses

Every real estate license states the licensee's name and type of license and must be prominently displayed in the place of business. All new licenses issued by the Idaho Real Estate Commission must be signed by the licensee. If a salesperson works out of a broker's branch office, his or her license will be displayed in that branch. A salesperson's license is mailed to the supervising broker at the office with which he or she will be affiliated.

License renewal (Sections 54-2029, D and E). Real estate licenses are renewed on a staggered schedule. A license expires every two years on the last day of the month of the licensee's birth date. Licensees who do not pay the renewal fee on or before the first day of the month following their birth month are subject to a fine and other conditions as described in the section entitled "Fees" in this chapter. The license of a broker, associate broker or salesperson who fails to renew promptly is suspended and the licensee must cease all real estate activities until the license is renewed.

Termination and transfer of a salesperson's license. When a salesperson changes affiliation from one broker to another, or when the supervising broker terminates a salesperson, that salesperson's wall license must be returned to the commission immediately along with a properly completed form and any required fee for transfer. This is usually done by the supervising broker but individual salespeople may deliver their own wall license to the commission for transfer. If the license is not available to the supervising broker for termination, the broker may send the commission a written notice of the termination by certified mail.

Termination of broker status. When an actively licensed broker changes his or her license status to one other than that of designated or individual broker, the broker must inform the commission immediately of the location of all trust accounts and transaction file records for which he or she was responsible. These records must be available for inspection by the commission for a period of three years following the year in which each transaction closed.

Surrender, suspension or revocation of a license. When a real estate broker or sales associate surrenders his or her license or is notified that the license is suspended or revoked, he or she must immediately forward the license to the commission.

Real Estate Contracts and Documents

The Idaho Real Estate License Law and Rules and Regulations of the Idaho Real Estate Commission include specific provisions regarding the documents involved in a real estate sales transaction.

Listing agreements. Any contract that promises payment of money or other valuable consideration as a commission for finding a purchaser for real estate must be in writing and signed by the owner of the property involved (or by a legal representative of the owner), as well as by the listing broker or the broker's agent. In addition, every listing must include a proper legal description of the property involved, the asking price and acceptable payment terms, the expiration date of the listing and the commission to be paid to the broker. Furthermore, the licensee who obtains the listing must, at that time, give a true copy of the agreement to the person or persons signing it.

Purchase and sales agreements. After a listing agreement is signed, the licensee has certain obligations regarding any known offers to purchase that are executed by prospective purchasers or any offers that may be pending. To begin with, a purchase and sales agreement is considered to be an offer to purchase with a receipt of earnest money, and the licensee must immediately give the prospective purchaser a copy of the agreement as a receipt for that earnest money. The licensee also must make sure that all terms and conditions of the proposed transaction are included in the purchase and sales agreement. In addition, the actual amount of earnest money received from the prospective purchaser and the form of payment must be specifically stated in the agreement.

The licensee is obligated to promptly deliver every written offer to purchase to the owner of the property involved. After the owner accepts an offer and signs the agreement, the licensee then delivers a true, executed copy of the document to the purchaser and the seller. If the offer is rejected, however, the document must be clearly marked "rejected," dated and retained in the broker's files.

Closing statement. At the closing of the transaction, the listing broker or designated broker is responsible for the accuracy of the closing statement and for delivery of a copy of the statement to the purchaser and the seller. The responsible broker must show proof of proper delivery by obtaining the buyer's and seller's signatures on the file copies of the closing statements or by maintaining a copy of any closing statement transmittal letters kept in files. If the transaction was closed in escrow and the buyer's and seller's signatures are not obtained, the responsible broker must maintain in his or her files a written certification by the escrow closing officer attesting that the closing documents were properly delivered. A sales associate may handle the closing of a transaction only when authorized by his or her supervising broker. If the transaction is a co-op sale between two or more brokers, the purchase and sales agreement must state which broker is responsible for closing the transaction. The broker must maintain copies of all documents pertaining to a transaction for three years after the year in which the transaction is closed. In the broker's records, transactions must be numbered and filed in sequence by transaction number or filed alphabetically.

Double contracts. IREC rules 4, 3,0 on Business Conduct Section of IREC rules and regulations specifically outlaws the practice of using double contracts in a real estate sales transaction. A *double contract* refers to any separate undisclosed agreement between buyer and seller that contradicts any part of the primary agreement or two separate purchase and sales agreements or loan applications concerning the same parcel of real estate, one stating the true purchase price and the other stating a larger purchase price. Such contracts are used to induce a lender (or loan guarantor) to make a loan commitment for a larger amount based on the larger, inflated purchase price quoted on the second document or to include items of personal property that cannot be financed by the lender. Any licensee found guilty of this act will be subject to disciplinary action by the commission, including suspension or revocation of his or her license.

Care and Handling of Funds (Sections 54-2049 and 54-2050)

All funds entrusted to a broker in connection with a real estate transaction must be placed in an approved escrow depository in Idaho or in a special trust fund checking account that the broker maintains in Idaho for this purpose. A broker may establish more than one trust fund account; each should be identified as to the type of activity for which funds will be accounted. The broker may deposit funds in an interest-bearing trust account of an insured Idaho depository if directed in writing by the parties to the transaction and if the broker maintains control of the funds so that they are available on demand. Approved escrow depositories as described in Rule 3,4,3 may also prepare the closing statement for the transaction. The broker is held personally responsible for these funds until they are disbursed and a full accounting is made to all parties to the transaction.

The money must be deposited on or before the next banking day after the broker receives it, except in situations where the purchase and sales agreement provides that a check given as earnest money is to be held for a specific length of time or to be deposited after the seller has accepted the buyer's offer, or where the agreement provides that the funds received by the broker are to be made payable to and held by a specified escrow closing agent. If any funds are to be deposited with some person, business or agent other than the broker handling the transaction (such as an attorney or escrow closing company), the broker must keep written instructions signed by the parties as to how such funds are to be deposited and disbursed. In addition, such funds must be deposited on or before the next banking day and the broker must retain a dated receipt in his or her file. A salesperson receiving earnest money deposits or other funds belonging to others in connection with a real estate transaction must immediately turn them over to the broker. *Entrusted funds never may be commingled (mixed in) with a real estate licensee's personal funds.* A broker is prohibited from depositing any funds in the trust account that were not received in connection with a real estate transaction for which he or she is acting as agent, with the exception of a maximum deposit of $100 as necessary to keep the trust account open.

Monies entrusted to a broker by a client may be disbursed only as provided by the terms of the purchase and sales agreement, on written authorization of both buyer and seller or by court order. A broker is not entitled to take any of the earnest money or other entrusted funds as part of his or her commission until the transaction in question has been completed, when the closing statements have been delivered to the parties and the seller has been paid the amount due as indicated in the closing statements. The purchase and sales agreement must provide for the disbursement of the earnest money if the transaction is not completed and such money is forfeited. If the transaction is not completed and the consideration is returned before it is deposited in the broker's account, a dated notation to this effect must appear on the copy of the earnest money agreement to be retained in the broker's files.

Record keeping. The Rules and Regulations describe the specific records a broker is required to keep regarding deposits and disbursements of entrusted funds. First, the broker must have a set of checks and deposit slips for the special bank account that indicates the broker's business name and address and clearly identifies the account as a "real estate trust account." Checks drawn on this account must be identified as to the specific transactions and retained by the broker along with any voided checks in numerical sequence. The broker also must keep a duplicate bank deposit book that shows the source of each deposit and the date and place it was deposited. In addition, the broker must keep a journal or record book of itemized deposits and disbursements of entrusted funds and an individual trust ledger sheet for each transaction that notes the details of the transaction and any entrusted funds taken in or paid out by the broker. A real estate trust fund account must be kept up to date. Ledger cards must be maintained in one location and not scattered throughout the broker's files. The files must be maintained in sequence, either by transaction number or in alphabetical order. The individual transaction trust ledger sheets must be kept in the broker's records for at least three calendar years after the year in which the transaction was closed. Any record-keeping system approved by the Idaho Real Estate Commission or its appointed representatives may be used instead of this system.

Trust account audits. The Idaho Real Estate Commission or its representative may make periodic investigations of brokers' trust fund accounts. If any deficiency or irregularity is discovered during such an investigation, the commission may order a complete audit of the account in question at the broker's expense.

Commissions

A person must obtain a real estate license before being entitled to collect a commission for engaging in real estate activities. In addition to this provision, Section 54-2039 of the license law makes it illegal for a licensee to pay part of a real estate commission to, or share a commission with, a person who does not have a real estate license. Furthermore, a sales associate is prohibited from accepting any compensation for engaging in real estate activities from any person except the broker with whom he or she is associated. A broker may not accept compensation from more than one party to a transaction without first informing all parties to the transaction of all the facts, in writing. The amount of commission earned by a broker in any real estate transaction is a matter to be decided between the broker and his or her principal. The Idaho Real Estate Commission does not set uniform rates of commission or recognize any agreement between brokers to standardize rates. Furthermore, the commission will not interfere in any disputes between licensees concerning commissions.

Other Provisions and Ethical Considerations

Title opinion. An Idaho real estate licensee may not state a personal opinion on the condition of the title to real estate that is involved in a transaction. In addition, a licensee may not discourage any party to a transaction from consulting an attorney.

Licensee's personal interest. Any licensee who directly, or indirectly through a third party, sells, purchases, acquires or intends to acquire for personal use any interest in real property or an option to purchase real property must make written disclosure of this situation to the owner and state that he or she is a real estate licensee.

Kickbacks and rebates. A licensee may not direct any parties to a transaction to a particular lender, escrow company or title company with the expectation of receiving a kickback or rebate from the lender or company, unless he or she first informs the parties to the transaction in writing of that expectation.

Advertising. Any advertisement of real property by an active licensee, whether for his or her own property or for property owned by others, must indicate that it is being made by a person engaged in the real estate business, not a private party. Every advertisement of property that is listed with a broker must be made under the broker's direct supervision, as provided in the listing agreement, and in the broker's business name; advertisements placed by a broker's branch offices also must clearly indicate the broker's business name. Advertising that only identifies a post office box number, a telephone number or a street address is not permitted.

SUSPENSION OR REVOCATION OF A LICENSE
AND IMPOSITION OF CIVIL PENALTY (Section 54-2040)

The Idaho Real Estate Commission may investigate the actions of any licensee who is suspected of performing one or more prohibited acts while engaging in real estate activities. Such an investigation may be instigated solely by the commission or it may be prompted by the verified written complaint of any person claiming to have been injured or defrauded by the actions of a real estate licensee. The real estate license of anyone who is found guilty of any number of acts may be suspended or revoked and a maximum fine of $1,000 imposed; if the license of a designated broker is suspended or revoked, the partnership or corporation he or she represents may lose its license and be fined a maximum of $2,000. The forbidden acts are:

1. making any fraudulent misrepresentations,

2. a continued or flagrant course of misrepresentation or making of false promises, whether through agents or salespeople,

3. failure to account for or remit any property or monies coming into his or her possession that belong to another,

4. failure to keep adequate records of all property transactions in which he or she acts in the capacity of real estate broker or real estate salesperson,

5. failure or refusal upon demand to disclose any information within his or her knowledge, or to produce any documents, books or records in the licensee's possession for inspection by the commission or its authorized representatives when acting within the jurisdiction or by authority of law,

6. employment of fraud, deception, misrepresentation, misstatement or any unlawful means in applying for or securing a license to act as a real estate broker or salesperson in the state of Idaho,

7. acting as a real estate broker or salesperson under an assumed name,

8. violation of any provision of Sections 54-2021 to 54-2053, Idaho Code, or any of the rules and regulations made or promulgated by the real estate commission, or final order of the commission,

9. any other conduct whether of the same or a different character than hereinabove specified that constitutes dishonest or dishonorable dealings, and

10. the use by a licensee of any provision allowing the licensee an option to purchase in any agreement authorizing or employing such licensee to sell, buy, list or exchange real estate for compensation or commission, except when such licensee, prior to or coincident with entering into such agreement, discloses in writing to the principal the purpose for which the property will be purchased, that the licensee is licensed and such other information as the commission may rule.

The commission also may temporarily suspend or permanently revoke a license if the holder is:

1. convicted of a felony in a state or federal court or is convicted of any crime involving moral turpitude. The record of conviction, or a certified copy thereof, certified by the clerk of the court or the judge in whose court the judgment was had shall be prima facie evidence of conviction in such cases.

2. declared insane by a court of competent jurisdiction. However, when a license has been revoked or suspended for this reason, the license may be reactivated by the commission when a declaration of sanity is made.

3. found to have a judgment entered against him or her in a civil action upon grounds of fraud, misrepresentation or deceit with reference to any transaction for which a license is required.

If the commission temporarily suspends or permanently revokes a license, and/or imposes a civil penalty, the commission may withhold execution of said suspension, revocation and/or civil penalty on such terms and for such time as it may prescribe.

In the event of the revocation or suspension of the broker's license issued to the designated broker of a partnership or corporation, the license issued to such partnership or corporation shall be revoked or suspended by the commission. However, the commission may withhold execution of the revocation or suspension on such terms and for such time as it may prescribe.

All civil penalties collected by the commission under the provisions of this chapter shall be deposited in the state treasury to the credit of the special real estate account established pursuant to Section 54-2037, Idaho Code.

Review (Section 54-2042)

Any person whose real estate license has been suspended or revoked by the commission has a right to request a review by the district court of the county in which he or she lives. The court will review the proceedings concerning the suspension or revocation.

Termination of Salesperson's Association for Prohibited Acts (Section 54-2047)

Whenever any licensee is discharged by a supervising broker for performing any prohibited act listed on the preceding pages, the broker must file a written statement of the facts in the case with the commission.

Legal Action Against License Law Violations (Sections 54-2043, 54-2051 and 54-2053)

The commission may bring charges in any court of competent jurisdiction against a person for violating the real estate license law. All violations are misdemeanors and are prosecuted by the prosecuting attorney of the county in which they took place. The commission also may request a court injunction (order) to prevent any person from violating any provision of the license law if there is cause to believe a violation will occur. In addition, members of the commission, or any person designated by rule, can administer oaths, certify to all official acts, issue subpoenas for attendance of witnesses and the production of books and papers, and, in civil cases, take the testimony of any person by deposition in any investigation or hearing in any part of the state in the manner prescribed for in the rules of procedure of the district court of this state. The fees of a witness who is subpoenaed will be paid either by the party who requests the witness or by funds appropriated for the commission's use.

THE REAL ESTATE INSPECTOR

Periodically a representative of the Idaho Real Estate Commission will visit a broker's office. The purpose of the inspector's visit is to find and correct problems before they become serious violations. He or she also answers licensees' questions and hears their recommendations regarding the real estate profession and the license law. The real estate broker who conducts his or her business activities according to the provisions of the license law and the principles of good business ethics will find these visits very beneficial.

The Inspector's Visit

Brokers are required to keep certain records of each transaction in their files for at least three calendar years after the year in which the transaction was closed. The inspector will examine all pending transactions, as well as some finalized sales, comparing the provisions of the purchase and sales agreement of each with the manner in which the transaction was closed. Any deposits and disbursements will be scrutinized to make sure that the account was handled properly and that the broker was authorized to make the disbursements. Prorations, title costs and other expense items will be checked for correctness. In addition the inspector will examine the licenses of all people who work out of the broker's office to make sure that they are current and properly displayed. Any violations will be noted and reported to the commission. The broker will be advised by the commission office of what action the commission has decided to take regarding such violations.

Cooperating with the Inspector

In expectation of the inspector's visit, the broker's files must be kept in good order so that the inspector can easily relate them to the proper trust accounting records. Failure to keep records as required by law is a serious violation that will prompt a more complete investigation of the broker's activities by the commission staff. Any attempt to hide or withhold information will not be tolerated; ignorance of the law is no excuse. In general the inspector's job is to help the broker and to advise the broker on any minor discrepancies. He or she is trained to do a thorough examination and will cooperate with the broker as much as possible under the law. The broker should be prepared to do the same.

When dealing with the inspector, however, the broker should remember that the inspector's authority and training are limited to the Idaho Real Estate License Law and the commission's Rules and Regulations. The inspector should not be expected to give advice or assistance on real estate problems that are outside this jurisdiction.

QUESTIONS

1. Which of the following persons must have a real estate broker's license in order to transact business?

   a. Wilfred Shannon, who owns a six-plex and personally manages the building, collects rents and shows the apartments to his prospective tenants
   b. Leslie Albers, who negotiates the sales of entire businesses, including their stock, equipment and buildings for a promised fee
   c. Frank Drew, superintendent of a large apartment building, who shows apartments to prospective tenants as part of his regular duties
   d. Wanda Sutton, who has her father's written authority to negotiate the sale of and convey a residence owned by him

2. The Idaho Real Estate Commission consists of:

   a. seven members.   c. four members.
   b. five members.   d. three members.

3. An applicant for a real estate license in Idaho must:

   a. have completed at least two years of college.
   b. be at least 21 years old.
   c. not have been convicted of a felony within five years of applying.
   d. not have had a real estate license revoked or suspended in any state for any reason.

4. Which of the following statements regarding the Idaho Real Estate Commission is *not* true?

   a. Members of the commission are selected by the Idaho Association of REALTORS®.
   b. The commission makes and enforces regulations that all real estate licensees must abide by.
   c. The examinations that must be taken by all applicants for real estate licensing are administered by an independent testing company.
   d. The operation of the commission's activities is administered by an executive director specifically hired for that purpose.

5. Which of the following statements regarding the licensing of corporations and partnerships as real estate brokers is true?

   a. All the officers or partners must qualify as brokers and pass the required written examination.
   b. The names and addresses of all officers, directors or partners must be submitted to the commission with the application.
   c. A separate fee must be paid to the commission office for each individual broker's license, in addition to the fee for the corporation's or partnership's license.
   d. All applicants must file an irrevocable consent agreement with the commission.

6. A person who obtains an Idaho reciprocal real estate license:

   a. must be licensed as a broker or salesperson in any state.
   b. must establish a principal place of business in Idaho or be licensed under a resident Idaho broker.
   c. need not take any written examination, provided he or she has passed a written examination to obtain a license in the state of residency.
   d. must file an irrevocable consent agreement with the commission.

7. Whenever the commission is required to satisfy a claim against a licensee with money from the Real Estate Recovery Account:

   a. the licensee may continue engaging in real estate activities under the commission's direct supervision.
   b. the licensee must repay the full amount plus interest to the account if his or her license is to be reinstated.
   c. the aggrieved party may later collect additional damages by forcing the sale of any property newly acquired by the defendant licensee.
   d. the licensee must thereafter pay $25 per year into the account when applying to renew his or her license.

8. After Nicholas Fargo purchased his new home, he discovered that broker Stuart Warbucks had deceived him regarding the condition of the property. Fargo sued Warbucks and obtained a judgment against him. In order to collect the judgment from the Real Estate Recovery Account, Fargo must:

   a. petition the commission to hold a hearing on the matter.
   b. file a Request for Recovery with the executive director of the commission.
   c. petition the court to direct payment from the account and then prove that the judgment cannot be collected from Warbucks in any other way.
   d. apply to the state treasurer for payment from the account.

9. A real estate license:

   a. is renewed every year.
   b. must be prominently displayed in the real estate office out of which the licensee works.
   c. must be carried by the licensee at all times.
   d. indicates the licensee's home address.

10. Associate broker Judi Rogers is not satisfied with the "unwritten" terms of her contract at Westphal and Company Real Estate and has decided to become associated with New Horizon Realty. Before Judi can begin actively selling for her broker at New Horizon Realty:

   a. The broker with Westphal and Company Real Estate must transfer Judi's license to New Horizon Realty.
   b. Judi's new broker must notify the commission of the change and send in the proper forms and fees.
   c. Judi must take her license with her to New Horizon Realty and notify the commission, within three days, of her transfer to a new location.
   d. Judi must have her license returned to the commission along with the proper fee and form signed by the broker of New Horizon Realty.

11. A listing agreement entered into by a broker need *not*:

   a. be in writing.
   b. be notarized.
   c. state the amount of the broker's commission.
   d. state a definite termination date.

12. Broker Eleanor Wrigley has obtained an offer to purchase a residence that is listed with her firm. After the buyers sign a purchase and sales agreement and Wrigley accepts their earnest money deposit, Wrigley must:

   a. deposit the earnest money in her personal checking account for safekeeping until the closing.
   b. complete a second earnest money agreement form that states an exaggerated selling price and give the second form to the buyers to present to the lender so that they will be certain to obtain sufficient financing for their purchase.
   c. immediately give the buyers a copy of the agreement as a receipt for their deposit.
   d. file the agreement in her records and, when she has obtained two or three other offers for the property, present them all to the sellers, who then may choose the best offer.

13. In any real estate sales transaction that a broker negotiates, the broker is *not* required to:

   a. inform the buyer of his or her personal opinion of the condition of the seller's title to the property.
   b. make sure that the written purchase and sales agreement includes all the terms of the parties' agreement.
   c. make sure that the closing statement is accurate and that a copy of it is delivered to both buyer and seller.
   d. keep copies of all documents involved in the transaction in his or her files for three years after the year in which the transaction was closed.

14. In Idaho, brokers are responsible for the closing of real estate sales transactions. A salesperson may be delegated to supervise the closing of a transaction:

   a. as part of his or her regular duties.
   b. only with the written consent of both buyer and seller.
   c. only when authorized by his or her supervising broker.
   d. only after obtaining written authorization from the Idaho Real Estate Commission.

15. The real estate inspector:

    a. is a newspaper, published by the Idaho Real Estate Commission, in which brokers can advertise real property for sale.
    b. is a trained professional who can be engaged to inspect a parcel of real estate and furnish a written report of the physical condition of the property.
    c. is a representative of the Idaho Real Estate Commission who periodically visits a broker's office to make sure that the broker is operating according to the provisions of the Real Estate License Law and the commission's Rules and Regulations.
    d. is a county official who examines documents for their validity before they are recorded by the county recorder.

16. The commission earned by a broker in a real estate sales transaction:

    a. is determined by agreement of the broker and his or her principal.
    b. may be shared with an unlicensed person, provided that such person aided the broker in bringing the buyer and seller together.
    c. must be deducted from the earnest money deposit and claimed by the broker as soon as the buyer and seller execute the purchase and sales agreement.
    d. is based on a schedule of commission rates set by the Idaho Real Estate Commission.

17. Broker Thomas Altman took a listing for a small office building owned by Donald Fine. Because the property is in excellent condition and produces a good, steady income, Altman's salesman has decided to purchase it himself as an investment. If Altman's salesman wishes to buy this property, he must:

    a. resign as Fine's agent and make an offer after Fine has retained another broker.
    b. have some third party purchase the property on his behalf so that Fine does not learn the true identity of the purchaser.
    c. obtain permission from the Idaho Real Estate Commission.
    d. inform Fine in writing that he is a licensee before making an offer.

18. In which of the following situations are the licensee's activities *not* cause for the suspension or revocation of his or her license?

    a. Salesperson Roberta Durning has been found guilty of income tax evasion.
    b. Broker Sam Warren, owner of Warren Realty, advertised some property for sale in the local newspaper. The ad listed Warren's home address and telephone number and gave his name as Sid Wilcox. Warren also used the name Sid Wilcox when negotiating with prospective purchasers of the property.
    c. Broker Bill Rossi obtained an offer to purchase a residence and accepted an earnest money deposit from the buyers; the sellers accepted the offer. The parties agreed to deposit the earnest money and close the transaction in escrow with the Homestead Title Insurance Company of Idaho acting as escrow agent. Rossi immediately deposited the earnest money with Homestead.
    d. Broker Abe Cotter accepted a listing for a property owned by the Schneiders. The listing agreement included an option for Cotter to purchase the property at the listing price of $40,000. After further inspection of the property, Cotter discovered that it was worth considerably more than the Schneiders were asking. He exercised his option and purchased the property without informing the Schneiders of its real worth, and later sold it for $50,000.

Real Estate Financing

In Idaho, a *lien theory* state, a mortgage may not be considered a conveyance, regardless of its terms or wording. For this reason, the holder of a mortgage cannot recover possession of the real estate upon the borrower's default without a judicial foreclosure sale.

PROMISSORY NOTES

The text includes a general discussion of the promissory note, one of two instruments executed by a borrower in connection with a mortgage or deed of trust loan. The notes usually used in real estate financing are *negotiable instruments*, which facilitate the holder's ability to transfer his or her right to payment to a third party. The Uniform Commercial Code, which governs negotiable instruments, defines one as a written, unconditional promise or order to pay a certain sum of money, either on demand or on a certain date, payable to order or bearer and signed by the maker.

The transfer may be accomplished by signing the negotiable note over to the third party or, in some cases, by merely delivering the instrument to another party. Endorsing the note over to a third party may be accomplished by a *blank endorsement*—the payee signing the back of the note. Another method is by *special endorsement;* a specific person is named as the new payee on the back and then the original payee signs. When the payee does not want to be liable to the new owner of the note for future payments by the maker, he or she can state the endorsement is *without recourse,* and the issue of future payments will be between the maker and the new owner of the note. If the new holder of the note has obtained the negotiable instrument in the ordinary course of business, before it is due, in good faith and for value, without knowledge that it has been previously dishonored and without notice of any defect or setoff at the time it was negotiated, then that transferee meets all the requisites to qualify as a *holder in due course*.

Types of Notes

Three types of promissory notes are generally used with mortgages and trust deeds. The payment plans required for all three types are described in the text. A *straight note* calls for periodic payments of interest with the principal to be paid at the end of the loan term. An *amortized note* requires a set periodic payment that is applied first to interest and the balance to principal over a number of years. An *installment note* calls for a set periodic payment on the principal plus an additional amount for the interest due on each payment.

TRUST DEEDS

In 1971 the Idaho legislature amended a 1957 law to authorize the use of trust deeds (deeds of trust) in real estate loans in which the property securing the debt is *not more than 20 acres or is within an incorporated city*. As discussed in the text, a trust deed is a three-party document involving the borrower, known in Idaho as the *grantor; the lender* or *beneficiary;* and the *trustee,* the third party to whom legal title to the real estate is conveyed by the deed of trust. Any one of the following persons or entities may serve as a trustee in Idaho:

1.   a member of the Idaho State Bar (attorney),

2.   a bank or savings and loan association authorized to conduct business under Idaho or federal law,

3.   a corporation authorized to conduct a trust business under Idaho or federal law, or

4.   a title insurance or abstract company authorized to transact business under Idaho law.

Because most trust deed loans are long term, a trustee who will be able to serve for a long period of time should be chosen. The business affairs of a financial institution or title company do not terminate upon the death of one officer, so the trusteeship of such an institution or company cannot be interrupted for this reason. In the event of the death, incapacity, disability or resignation of an individual trustee, the beneficiary may name another qualified trustee to acquire the same power and authority of the original trustee. In the event of a breach or default of the trust deed, the trustee has the *power of sale* to foreclose and sell the property without court proceedings.

Examples of a typical trust deed form used in Idaho and the note that is used with it are included at the end of the chapter.

Repayment of Mortgage or Trust Deed Loans

When a real estate loan secured by a trust deed has been completely repaid, the beneficiary certifies this fact by completing the *request for reconveyance* form located on the reverse side of the trust deed and delivering it to the trustee together with the paid promissory note. After receiving this written request from the beneficiary, the trustee executes and delivers a *deed of reconveyance* to the grantor conveying the property back to the grantor with the same rights and powers that the trustee was given under the trust deed.

The deed of reconveyance (described in the text as a release deed) should be acknowledged and recorded in the public record of the county in which the property is located.

When a real estate loan secured by a mortgage has been completely repaid, the mortgage may be released in one of two ways. First, it may be released by recording a separate satisfaction of mortgage, signed by the mortgagee and stating that the mortgage loan has been paid, satisfied or discharged. Second, a notation acknowledging the release, or satisfaction, may be entered in the margin of the recorded mortgage document and signed by the mortgagee in the presence of the county recorder. A marginal release is the exception, not the rule, on property transactions in Idaho.

Release clause. The concept of blanket mortgage and trust deed loans is described in the text. The *release clause* in a blanket mortgage document or trust deed enables the lender to release portions of the property from the blanket encumbrance as those portions of the debt are repaid. In the case of a trust deed, the lender instructs the trustee to execute and deliver a *partial reconveyance* to the grantor each time a portion of the debt is released.

Assumption of Mortgage and Trust Deed Loans

The subject of real estate loan assumptions is discussed in the text. Usually when a purchaser of real estate assumes the seller's existing loan, the lender charges the purchaser a fee for transferring the loan. This is known as an *assumption fee* and is expressed in points, or assumption points.

Frequently when a real estate loan is made, the lender wishes to prevent some future purchaser of the property from being able to assume that loan, particularly at its old rate of interest. For this reason some lenders include an *alienation (resale) clause* or *due-on-sale clause*. An alienation clause provides that, upon the sale of the property by the borrower, the lender has the choice of either declaring the entire debt to be immediately due and owing or permitting the buyer to assume the loan. Sometimes an acceleration clause, as discussed in the text, also is employed for this purpose. By utilizing such clauses, the lender can choose to call the loan in the event of a sale and effectively reduce the number of notes with low interest rates that it holds and at the same time qualify new home purchasers on their income and paying ability before allowing them to assume an existing loan.

Trust Deed Foreclosure Procedure

If the grantor (or some person who owes an obligation, the performance of which is secured by a recorded trust deed) defaults, the trustee may foreclose on the grantor by advertising and holding a sale of the property or by instituting legal proceedings to recover the debt through the mortgage (judicial) foreclosure procedure. The trustee may exercise his or her power of sale provided that no such action, suit or proceeding has been instituted. If such a suit has been instituted, the trustee may advertise and sell the property only if that suit has been dismissed by the court.

Notice of default. In order for the trustee to advertise and sell the property, the trustee (or the beneficiary) must file a *notice of default* with the county recorder identifying the specific trust deed involved and the nature of the breach and expressing the trustee's intention to sell the property to satisfy the obligation. This notice must be recorded in all counties in which the property or sections of the property are located. In addition a copy of the notice must be sent to every person who has filed a request with the lender to receive one or has recorded a request for notice of default with county recorder.

Notice of sale. After recording the notice of default, and at least 120 days before the date of the sale, the trustee must notify the following persons or their legal representatives by certified or registered mail at their last known addresses:

1.   the grantor,

2.   any person who has acquired the grantor's interest, provided that such successor's interest is indicated in the public record, the successor is in possession of the property or the trustee has actual knowledge of the interest,

3.   any lessee or other person in possession of the property, and

4.   any person holding a lien or interest in the property that arose after the trustee's interest, provided that such lien or interest appears in the public record or the trustee has actual knowledge of it.

The disability, incompetency, insanity or death of any person who should receive a notice of the sale does not prevent the trustee from going ahead with the sale.

The following items should be included in the notice of sale:

1. the names of the grantor, beneficiary and trustee,

2. a description of the property covered by the trust deed,

3. the location of the recorded trust deed—book and page number of the mortgage records or the recorded instrument number,

4. a description of the default,

5. the unpaid balance of the debt, and

6. the date, time and place of the sale.

In addition a copy of the notice of sale must be published in a newspaper of general circulation in each county in which a section of the property is located. This advertisement of the sale must be published once each week for four successive weeks, with the last publication at least 30 days before the sale.

The sale. The trustee's sale must be held at a designated time between 9:00 A.M. and 4:00 P.M., Standard Time, and at a designated place in the county or one of the counties where the property is located.

A recent revision of Idaho's deed of trust statute allows for a postponement of a foreclosure sale past the date on which it was scheduled. Some lenders have seized upon foreclosure sale postponement as a technique for negotiating a repayment schedule with the borrower while keeping the borrower in what amounts to near perpetual default. By using this technique, lenders who have reached an agreement with a borrower for repayment avoid having to go through an additional 120-day period from notice to sale date. They are never more than 30 days away from a foreclosure sale. Despite the pressure of a possible foreclosure every 30 days, postponement provides a means by which borrowers who are unable to cure a default within the statutory period can still preserve their property.

The trustee's attorney may conduct the sale. The property is auctioned off to the highest bidder. It may be sold as one parcel or divided into sections and sold as two or more separate parcels. Anyone, including the beneficiary under the trust deed, may bid on the property. After the sale and upon receiving the purchaser's payment for the property, the trustee executes and delivers a *trustee's deed* to the purchaser. A trustee's deed conveys to the purchaser *all* interest that the defaulted grantor had in the property. The purchaser is entitled to take possession of the property ten days after the sale.

Trustee sale proceeds. The trustee must apply the proceeds from the sale as follows:

1. to pay the expenses of the sale, including reasonable fees for the trustee and the attorney,

2. to pay off the debt secured by the trust deed,

3. to pay off any liens recorded after the trust deed in the order of their priority, and

4. to pay any surplus funds from the sale to the defaulted grantor or his or her successor in interest.

If, after deducting expenses, the proceeds of the sale are not enough to cover the outstanding balance of the trust deed debt, the beneficiary is entitled to a *money judgment*, or deficiency judgment, as described in the text. Any such personal judgment must be sought within three months after the sale.

Mortgage Foreclosure Procedure

When mortgagors default, lenders must institute foreclosure proceedings under the *one-action rule*. This rule calls for a combined recovery of a debt and/or enforcement of a right secured by a mortgage in one action; no money judgment can be forced until the lender has foreclosed and the sale proceeds are insufficient to repay the lender. The mortgagee files a foreclosure suit that names all persons having a recorded interest in the property and requests *a sheriff's sale* of the property. At the court's direction, the sale is advertised. At the auction the highest bidder for the property receives a *sheriff's deed*.

Redemption

The equity of redemption enables a defaulted mortgagor or grantor to redeem his or her property by paying all monies owed on the loan plus expenses at any time before the sheriff's or trustee's sale. Idaho law also grants a defaulted mortgagor a time in which to redeem the property *after* a sale. The *statutory redemption period is one year after a sheriff's sale to foreclose a mortgage*, if the property sold consisted of *more than 20 acres*; *six months*, if the property sold consisted of *20 acres or less*. During this period, the lender holds legal title to the property by holding a sheriff's certificate of sale. At the foreclosure sale, if the lender (or some other party) acquires the property, that party cannot market the property until the redemption period expires, or without obtaining the debtor's release of his or her right of redemption.

In a proceeding to foreclose on a deed of trust in Idaho, the trustor may stop the foreclosure proceedings by paying the delinquent amount of payments plus any costs incurred in the foreclosure process, which reinstates the loan. This action to reinstate the loan must be done within 115 days from the date the formal notice of default was recorded. After the trustee's sale, the trustor has *no right* to redeem the property from the purchaser. The trustee's sale may not be held any earlier than 120 days after the date of the filing of the notice of default.

Although mortgages *must* be foreclosed judicially, deeds of trust *may* be foreclosed judicially; in either case, the one-action rule applies. If a deed of trust is foreclosed judicially, a payment of funds equal to the defaulted amount would not cure the default. Standard note, mortgage and deed of trust provisions require that upon default the entire indebtedness may become accelerated and due immediately at the lender's discretion.

Deed in Lieu of Foreclosure

The lender and the debtor may decide to satisfy the mortgage obligation by passing a *deed in lieu of foreclosure* to the lender; however, this action has the same result as an actual judicial foreclosure. Lenders generally use great caution before accepting a deed in lieu of foreclosure; the property may be subject to junior liens that could be discharged only by payment or by a notice and sale at some later date.

USURY AND THE UNIFORM CONSUMER CREDIT CODE (S15-5)

The 1983 Amended Idaho Code does not limit a maximum rate for usury when the rate of interest is expressly agreed to between parties in writing. With no expressed contract, 12 percent annual interest is allowed, according to Section 28-22-104 of the Idaho Code.

Subdividers who sell real estate or licensees who finance their commission on installment contracts (carryback financing) must be constantly alert to whether their sales constitute *consumer credit sales,* which are regulated by the Idaho Department of Finance. The law provides for severe penalties for failure to comply with statutory notification, disclosure and other requirements in connection with consumer credit sales. Section 28-41-301 of the Idaho Code defines *regulated credit sales* (item 35) as a sale of goods, services or an interest in land in which: (a) credit is granted either in conformance with a seller credit card or by a seller who regularly engages in credit transactions of the same kind; and (b) the debt is payable in installments or a finance charge is made. Section 28-46-201 of the Idaho Code describes notification and fees for regulated lenders, licensing and related provisions.

Points and late charges. Many lenders charge the borrower a fee known as points at the loan's inception in addition to the stated interest rate on the face of the note. A point, usually one percent of the loan principal, may be considered prepaid interest. Idaho borrowers using VA-guaranteed or FHA-insured loans were the first in the state to pay points. Later, points became a convenient method for many lenders to charge prepaid interest to compensate for low interest rates and provide a better return on their investments. If such points are, in fact, a bona fide service charge that can be justified or if they are actual brokerage or commitment fees, they are not considered prepaid interest to which the usury law applies.

Late charges are penalty fees charged by some institutional lenders to mortgagors who make their installment payments after the due date. Late charges are usually a specified percentage of the remaining unpaid principal.

Figure 14/15.1 Deed of Trust

DEED OF TRUST

THIS DEED OF TRUST, Made this   day of   19

BETWEEN

                                                                                                    herein called GRANTOR,

whose address is

PIONEER TITLE COMPANY OF CANYON COUNTY, an Idaho corporation, herein called TRUSTEE, whose address is 901 12th Ave. South, Nampa, Idaho 83651, and

                                        herein called BENEFICIARY, whose address is

WITNESSETH: That Grantor does hereby irrevocably GRANT, BARGAIN, SELL AND CONVEY TO TRUSTEE IN TRUST, WITH POWER OF SALE, that property in the County of   State of Idaho, described as follows, and containing not more than twenty acres:

TOGETHER WITH the rents, issues and profits thereof; SUBJECT, HOWEVER, to the right, power and authority hereinafter given to and conferred upon Beneficiary to collect and apply such rents, issues and profits.

For the Purpose of Securing payment of the indebtedness evidenced by a promissory note, of even date herewith, executed by Grantor in the sum of

_____ Dollars, ($_____)

final payment due _____

and to secure payment of all such further sums as may hereafter be loaned or advanced by the Beneficiary herein to the Grantor herein, or any or either of them, while record owner of present interest, for any purpose, and of any notes, drafts or other instruments representing such further loans, advances or expenditures together with interest on all such sums at the rate therein provided. Provided, however, that the making of such further loans, advances or expenditures shall be optional with the Beneficiary, and provided, further, that it is the express intention of the parties to this Deed of Trust that it shall stand as continuing security until paid for all such advances together with interest thereon.

A. To protect the security of this Deed of Trust, Grantor agrees:

1. To keep said property in good condition and repair; not to remove or demolish any building thereon; to complete or restore promptly and in good and workmanlike manner any building which may be constructed, damaged or destroyed thereon and to pay when due all claims for labor performed and materials furnished therefor; to comply with all laws affecting said property or requiring any alterations or improvements to be made thereon; not to commit or permit waste thereof; not to commit, suffer or permit any act upon said property in violation of law; to cultivate, irrigate, fertilize, fumigate, prune and do all other acts which from the character or use of said property may be reasonably necessary, the specific enumerations herein not excluding the general.

2. To provide, maintain and deliver to Beneficiary fire insurance satisfactory to and with loss payable to Beneficiary. The amount collected under any fire or other insurance policy may be applied by Beneficiary upon any indebtedness secured hereby and in such order as Beneficiary may determine, or at option of Beneficiary the entire amount so collected or any part thereof may be released to Grantor. Such application or release shall not cure or waive any default or notice of default hereunder or invalidate any act done pursuant to such notice.

3. To appear in and defend any action or proceeding purporting to affect the security hereof or the rights or powers of Beneficiary or Trustee; and to pay all costs and expenses, including cost of evidence of title and attorney's fees in a reasonable sum, in any such action or proceeding in which Beneficiary or Trustee may appear.

4. To pay: at least ten days before delinquency all taxes and assessments affecting said property, when due; all encumbrances, charges and liens, with interest, on said property or any part thereof, which appear to be prior or superior hereto; all costs, fees and expenses of this Trust. In addition to the payments due in accordance with the terms of the note hereby secured the Grantor shall at the option, and on demand of the Beneficiary, pay each month 1/12 of the estimated annual taxes, assessments, insurance premiums, maintenance and other charges upon the property, nevertheless in trust for Grantor's use and benefit and for the payment by Beneficiary of any such items when due. Grantor's failure so to pay shall constitute a default under this trust.

5. To pay immediately and without demand all sums expended by Beneficiary or Trustee pursuant to the provisions hereof, with interest from date of expenditure at eight per cent per annum.

6. Should Grantor fail to make any payment or to do any act as herein provided, then Beneficiary or Trustee, but without obligation so to do and without notice to or demand upon Grantor and without releasing Grantor from any obligation hereof, may: make or do the same in such manner and to such extent as either may deem necessary to protect the security hereof, Beneficiary or Trustee being authorized to enter upon said property for such purposes; appear in and defend any action or proceeding purporting to affect the security hereof or the rights or powers of Beneficiary or Trustee; pay, purchase, contest or compromise any encumbrance, charge or lien which in the judgment of either appears to be prior or superior hereto; and, in exercising any such powers, or in enforcing this Deed of Trust by judicial foreclosure, pay necessary expenses, employ counsel and pay his reasonable fees.

B. It is mutually agreed that:

1. Any award of damages in connection with any condemnation for public use of or injury to said property or any part thereof is hereby assigned and shall be paid to Beneficiary who may apply or release such moneys received by him in the same manner and with the same effect as above provided for disposition of proceeds of fire or other insurance.

2. By accepting payment of any sum secured hereby after its due date, Beneficiary does not waive his right either to require prompt payment when due of all other sums so secured or to declare default for failure so to pay.

3. At any time or from time to time, without liability therefor and without notice, upon written request of Beneficiary and presentation of this Deed and said note for endorsement, and without affecting the personal liability of any person for payment of the indebtedness secured hereby, Trustee may: reconvey all or any part of said property; consent to the making of any map or plat thereof; join in granting any easement thereon; or join in any extension agreement or any agreement subordinating the lien or charge hereof.

4. Upon written request of Beneficiary stating that all sums secured hereby have been paid, and upon surrender of this Deed and said note to Trustee for cancellation and retention and upon payment of its fees, Trustee shall reconvey, without warranty, the property then held hereunder. The recitals in any reconveyance executed under this deed of trust of any matters or facts shall be conclusive proof of the truthfulness thereof. The grantee in such reconveyance may be described as "the person or persons legally entitled thereto."

5. As additional security, Grantor hereby gives to and confers upon Beneficiary the right, power and authority, during the continance of these Trusts, to collect the rents, issues and profits of said property, reserving unto Grantor the right, prior to any default by Grantor in payment of any indebtedness secured hereby or in performance of any agreement hereunder, to collect and retain such rents, issues and profits as they become due and payable. Upon any such default, Beneficiary may at any time without notice, either in person, by agent, or by a receiver to be appointed by a court, and without regard to the adequacy of any security for the indebtedness hereby secured, enter upon and take possession of said property or any part thereof, in his own name sue for or otherwise collect such rents, issues and profits, including those past due and unpaid, and apply the same, less costs and expenses of operation and collection, including reasonable attorney's fees, upon any indebtedness secured hereby, and in such order as Beneficiary may determine. The entering upon and taking possession of said property, the collection of such rents, issues and profits and the application thereof as aforesaid, shall not cure or waive any default or notice of default hereunder or invalidate any act done pursuant to such notice.

6. Upon default by Grantor in payment of any indebtedness secured hereby or in performance of any agreement hereunder, all sums secured hereby shall immediately become due and payable at the option of the Beneficiary. In the event of default, Beneficiary shall execute or cause the Trustee to execute a written notice of such default and of his election to cause to be sold the herein described property to satisfy the obligations hereof, and shall cause such notice to be recorded in the office of the recorder of each county wherein said real property or some part thereof is situated.

Pioneer Title Company

Figure 14/15.1 Deed of Trust (Continued)

Notice of sale having been given as then required by law, and not less than the time then required by law having elapsed, Trustee, without demand on Grantor, shall sell said property at the time and place fixed by it in said notice of sale, either as a whole or in separate parcels and in such order as it may determine, at public auction to the highest bidder for cash in lawful money of the United States, payable at time of sale. Trustee shall deliver to the purchaser its deed conveying the property so sold, but without any covenant or warranty express or implied. The recitals in such deed of any matters or facts shall be conclusive proof of the truthfulness thereof. Any person, including Grantor, Trustee, or Beneficiary, may purchase at such sale.

After deducting all costs, fees and expenses of Trustee and of this Trust, including cost of evidence of title and reasonable counsel fees in connection with sale, Trustee shall apply the proceeds of sale to payment of: all sums expended under the terms hereof, not then repaid, with accrued interest at eight per cent per annum; all other sums then secured hereby; and the remainder, if any, to the person or persons legally entitled thereto.

7. This Deed applies to, inures to the benefit of, and binds all parties hereto, their heirs, legatees, devisees, administrators, executors, successors and assigns. The term Beneficiary shall mean the holder and owner of the note secured hereby; or, if the note has been pledged, the pledgee thereof. In this Deed, whenever the context so requires, the masculine gender includes the feminine and/or neuter, and the singular number includes the plural.

8. Trustee is not obligated to notify any party hereto of pending sale under any other Deed of Trust or of any action or proceeding in which Grantor, Beneficiary or Trustee shall be a party unless brought by Trustee.

9. In the event of dissolution or resignation of the Trustee, the Beneficiary may substitute a trustee or trustees to execute the trust hereby created, and when any such substitution has been filed for record in the office of the Recorder of the county in which the property herein described is situated, it shall be conclusive evidence of the appointment of such trustee or trustees, and such new trustee or trustees shall succeed to all of the powers and duties of the trustee or trustees named herein.

Request is hereby made that a copy of any Notice of Default and a copy of any Notice of Sale hereunder be mailed to the Grantor at his address hereinbefore set forth.

_____

_____

STATE OF IDAHO, COUNTY OF _____

On this _____ day of _____, 19____
before me, a Notary Public in and for said State, personally appeared

Known to me to be the person___ whose name _____
subscribed to the within instrument, and acknowledged to me that
_____ executed the same.

_____
Notary Public,

Residing at _____, Idaho.

Commission Expires _____

STATE OF IDAHO, COUNTY OF _____

I HEREBY CERTIFY That this instrument was filed for record at the
request of _____

at _____ minutes past _____ o'clock ____M.,
this _____ day of _____,
19, _____, in my office, and duly recorded in Book _____
of Mortgages at page _____

_____
Ex-Officio Recorder.

By _____
Deputy.

Fees: $ _____

Mail to: _____

DEED OF TRUST
WITH POWER OF SALE

GRANTOR

Pioneer Title Company of Canyon County
TRUSTEE

BENEFICIARY

Dated _____, 19____

Pioneer Title Company of Canyon County
901 12th Ave. South
NAMPA, ID 83651
(208) 466-8100

REQUEST FOR FULL RECONVEYANCE
TO BE USED ONLY WHEN NOTE HAS BEEN PAID.

_____, Idaho, _____ 19 _____

To PIONEER TITLE COMPANY OF CANYON COUNTY, Trustee:

The undersigned is the legal owner and holder of all indebtedness secured by the within Deed of Trust. All sums secured thereby have been fully paid. You are hereby requested and directed to cancel all evidences of indebtedness secured by said Deed of Trust and to reconvey, without warranty, the estate now held by you under the same.

Deliver to: _____

THE PROMISSORY NOTE OR NOTES, AND ANY EVIDENCES OF FURTHER AND/OR ADDITIONAL ADVANCES MUST BE PRESENTED WITH THIS REQUEST.

Figure 14/15.1 Deed of Trust (Continued)

$ _____   Idaho, _____   , 19 ___

I/We promise to pay to the order of   , at

Idaho, _____   DOLLARS,

payable in lawful money of the United States of America, with interest thereon in like money, from and

after _____   until paid, at the rate of _____   per cent per annum.

Principal and Interest to be paid as follows:

I/We agree that in case of default in the payment of any said installments, such unpaid installment shall bear interest from the date of such maturity until paid at the legal rate per annum, and that if any one of said installments or interest due hereon is not paid within ten (10) days after the same becomes due and payable, the whole of the principal sum then remaining unpaid, together with the interest that shall have accrued thereon, shall forthwith become due and payable at the election of the holder of this note, without notice. If action is commenced to enforce payment of this note, I/We agree to pay such sums as the court may affix as attorneys' fees. The maker ___ and endorser ___ hereon jointly and severally waive presentment for payment, demand, protest and notice of protest of non-payment of this note.

No. _____   _____

Due _____

PIONEER TITLE COMPANY
OF CANYON COUNTY
901 12th AVE. SOUTH, NAMPA, IDAHO 83651

QUESTIONS

1. A promissory note is negotiable when:

   a. it includes an alienation clause.
   b. it cannot be prepaid without penalty.
   c. the person who will collect payment on the note can transfer his or her right to collect to another party.
   d. the maker's debt may be assumed by another party.

2. Financier Arnold Kuppenheimer loaned $40,000 to Martin and Sylvia Wayne, who are opening a new restaurant. The promissory note executed by the Waynes states, "Pay to Bearer, the sum of forty thousand and no/100 dollars ($40,000.00)." Three months later, Kuppenheimer needed cash for some other project, so he sold the Waynes' note to Howard Luft, an associate who was interested in a long-term investment. In order to transfer his rights under the note to Luft, Kuppenheimer had to:

   a. give the note to Luft.
   b. have the Waynes execute a new note to Luft and destroy the original note.
   c. sign the note over to Luft.
   d. execute an endorsement agreement naming Luft as the official payee.

3. Deborah Reardon borrowed some money from the local bank to finance some needed repairs to her farm. The note that Reardon signed calls for her to make a monthly payment of $200 on the principal, plus interest at the rate of 9 percent per year. This is a(n):

   a. amortized note.
   b. straight note.
   c. installment note.
   d. balloon note.

4. Currently, the outstanding balance of Deborah Reardon's loan, as described in question 3, is $16,000. What is the total amount due for her next monthly payment?

   a. $320   c. $220
   b. $300   d. $200

5. A person who obtains a real estate loan secured by a trust deed is known as a:

   a. holder in due course.
   b. trustee.
   c. beneficiary.
   d. trustor.

6. In Idaho, real estate loans secured by trust deeds may be made, provided that the property given as security is:

   a. one acre or less.
   b. five acres or less.
   c. 15 acres or less.
   d. 20 acres or less.

7. Which of the following persons or entities may *not* serve as the trustee of a trust deed loan in Idaho?

   a. A real estate broker
   b. A title insurance company
   c. An attorney
   d. A savings and loan association

8. Several years ago, when Alan and Celia Smith obtained a trust deed loan from the Hometown National Bank, attorney Alexander Burns agreed to serve as trustee. Because the Smiths have neglected to make the last six payments on the loan, the bank has declared them to be in default and requested that Burns sell the property to repay the Smiths' obligation. The first step Burns must take to exercise his power of sale is to:

   a. schedule a time and place for the sale.
   b. record a notice of default in the county in which the property is located.
   c. notify the Smiths of the impending sale.
   d. notify the Smiths' other creditors of the impending sale.

9. In the situation described in question 8, the person who purchases the Smiths' property at the foreclosure sale will receive a:

   a. deed of reconveyance.
   b. release deed.
   c. sheriff's deed.
   d. trustee's deed.

10. In Idaho, the right of the trustor to redeem a property that has been foreclosed upon through a trustee's sale, must be exercised within:

    a. 115 days.
    b. 120 days.
    c. six months on 20 acres or less.
    d. No time after trustee's sale

11. The trustor may retain the property upon payment, to the lender, of all back payments and reasonable costs of foreclosure within:

    a. 115 days.
    b. 120 days.
    c. six months.
    d. Trustor can't stop sale.

16

Leases

Under Idaho law there are certain legal relationships between landlords and tenants. In addition to these legal relations, the parties to the lease or rental agreement can establish other arrangements. In normal situations the terms of a lease agreement are binding on all parties to the agreement and are enforceable in a court of law. The general principles covered by Idaho law can be modified or supplemented by the terms of the specific lease agreement.

LEASE AGREEMENTS

A lease agreement can be either oral or written. It is strongly recommended that all lease agreements be in writing, no matter the length of period. Because the lease agreement is a contract, it must contain all of the essential elements of a contract. The courts use state statutes and certain implied covenants and terms when dealing with all leases, whether or not the lease is in writing.

Written Lease Agreements

Before either party signs a lease agreement, all questions and changes in the terms of the agreement should be resolved. An oral statement contrary to the terms of the written lease agreement cannot be relied on. *Idaho's Statute of Frauds requires all leases of more than one year be in writing to be enforceable in a court of law.*

The other requirements of a valid written lease include consideration, signatures and legally competent parties. Consideration is normally the rent. The lease should spell out when the rent is to be paid, which generally is at the beginning of the period. If the lease agreement does not specify when rent is due, it will not be due until the end of the lease period. This could create added risk for the landlord, who would be unable to demand payment until the expiration of the lease period.

To be valid, the written lease agreement must be signed by the landlord (lessor). The tenant (lessee) need not sign the lease agreement, even though it is highly recommended. Acceptance by the tenant will be implied by his or her action, such as the payment of rent or taking possession of the property.

All of the standard lease terms discussed in the main text should be included in all written lease agreements.

Oral Lease Agreements

If the terms of the lease have been agreed on, a legally binding oral lease agreement may exist. The greatest difficulty encountered with an oral lease is proving what specific terms were agreed to.

Most oral lease agreements result in periodic tenancy. That is, the parties agree that the tenant will pay rent on a periodic basis in return for the landlord giving possession of the property to the tenant. The period can be for any agreed-upon length and will be equal to the period for which the payment is made.

THE RIGHTS AND RESPONSIBILITIES OF LANDLORD AND TENANT PROVIDED FOR BY IDAHO LAW

Idaho statutes provide for certain rights and require certain duties of both the landlord and the tenant in residential lease situations, regardless of whether a written lease agreement exists.

Possession

The tenant has the right to possession of the property during the term of the lease agreement; the landlord has the right to have possession of the property returned upon expiration of the term. However, the tenant does not vacate the property at the end of the term, the landlord is *prohibited* from locking the tenant out without a court order. The landlord is required by Idaho law to give certain notice to the tenant and, if required, to institute formal legal proceedings to regain possession of the property.

Entry by the Landlord

Idaho laws do not speak specifically to the landlord's right to enter the premises, so the lease agreement must spell out the rights of the landlord. The lease should allow the landlord to enter the property to make repairs, to inspect for damage, to show the property to potential purchasers and prospective new tenants. If such entry is at a reasonable time and in a reasonable manner, there should be no problem, provided the lease agreement covers entry.

If the lease agreement does not address the landlord's right to enter, the landlord should notify the tenant as to the necessity for entry and request permission to enter at a reasonable time and in a reasonable manner.

The landlord probably has the right to enter for inspection of the property under two situations:

1. If the landlord has reasonable cause to believe that damage is occurring to the property, the landlord probably has the right to enter to inspect for such damage. Arrangements for entry should be made with the tenant, if at all possible.

2. If a tenant is in default in the rent and has been absent from the premises for a considerable period of time, the landlord probably has the right to enter and inspect. This situation should be provided for in the terms of the lease agreement to resolve any possible conflicts.

Security Deposits

Under Idaho law a security deposit is for purposes other than the payment of rent. The lease agreement must specify the amount of the security deposit and what it can be used for. The security deposit *cannot* be used for payment of rent unless the lease agreement or deposit receipt clearly indicates in writing that it will be used for payment of rent. The security deposit cannot be used to cover normal wear and tear. Normal wear and tear is defined as the deterioration that occurs based on the use for which the space is intended and without negligence, carelessness, accident, misuse or abuse of the premises or contents by the tenants, their family or their guests.

If the landlord finds it necessary to use the security deposit, Idaho law requires the landlord to provide the tenant with a signed statement as to the expenditures required, the amount to be retained and the purpose for which the amount retained was used. This signed statement and the remaining amount of the security deposit, if any, or the full amount of the deposit, must be returned to the tenant within 21 days after the tenant surrenders the premises. In the original lease agreement the landlord and tenant can agree to extend this period up to 30 days, but for no longer.

The tenant is protected when the landlord refuses to comply with the requirements concerning security deposits. The tenant must first notify the landlord in writing of the violation and demand compliance. The landlord must be allowed three days to either refund the deposit or provide the necessary statement. After three days the tenant can institute a formal legal proceeding to require return of the security deposit. This lawsuit can be brought either in the district court with the aid of an attorney or in small claims court without the assistance of an attorney if the amount is not too large. If the tenant is successful, the court may award damages up to the amount of *three times* the security deposit.

Care of the Property

Safeguarding the property and ensuring that damage does not occur is one of a tenant's main responsibilities. A tenant will be held responsible and must pay for any damage that occurs due to tenant negligence or that of family members or guests.

The landlord is obligated to provide reasonable waterproofing and water protection and also to provide premises that are not hazardous to health and safety. A landlord who provides electrical, plumbing, heating, ventilating, cooling or sanitary facilities must maintain them in good working order.

Tenant's Property

Upon termination of the lease agreement, the tenant has a right to remove personal property as long as such removal does not damage the premises. If the tenant's property has become part of the landlord's real property, it cannot be removed.

If a tenant leaves property of value behind after vacating the premises, the landlord has no legal right to *immediately* dispose of the property. In fact the landlord has an obligation to reasonably safeguard the property until it can be disposed of properly. The tenant may reclaim the property or the landlord can dispose of it in accordance with the abandoned or unclaimed property laws of the state of Idaho.

Idaho law does *not* provide for a landlord's lien on property that belongs to a tenant. A lease agreement could contain a provision for the landlord to have a lien right on the tenant's property. The courts have upheld this type of lien right as long as the tenant knowingly and voluntarily enters into and understands the consequences of such an agreement.

Rent Increases

Proper notice is required before rent can be increased. A written notice must be given at least 15 days before the end of the term and prior to the date the rent increase is to become effective on all periodic tenancies. When the lease agreement, either written or oral, specifies the amount of the rent for a set time period, the rent cannot be increased during that period.

OTHER CHANGES IN LEASE AGREEMENT TERMS

None of the terms of a lease agreement for a specified time period can be changed unless both parties to the agreement consent to the proposed changes. Any changes made should be in writing as a modification to the lease agreement or be incorporated in an entirely new lease agreement.

The landlord may change the terms of the lease agreement in a periodic tenancy by giving the tenant written notice of changes at least 15 days before the end of the period and before the changes are to become effective. If the tenant continues to rent for the following period, the changes in the landlord's notice will automatically become effective for the new period.

Transfer of Property

During the term of the lease period, the owner has the right to sell the property. The lease cannot prevent the sale; however, the sale is made *subject to* the lease. This means that the buyer (new owner) must recognize the existence of the lease and honor the lease for the remainder of the term. The only exception is if the lease contains a sales clause term, which allows the new landlord to terminate the lease agreement.

The tenant has certain additional rights, unless a right is specifically prohibited by the provisions of the lease. These additional rights include the rights to assign, sublease or novate the lease interest. These three situations create different levels of liability for the first tenant. In the case of an assignment the first tenant is not relieved of responsibility to pay rent and in fact is secondarily liable to pay. Under the sublease situation the first tenant is primarily liable along with the new tenant. A novation allows the first tenant to terminate his or her liability under the old lease by replacing the old lease agreement with a new lease agreement with a new tenant.

TERMINATION BECAUSE OF BREACH OF LEASE TERMS

Landlord's Remedies

Idaho law specifically speaks to the requirements that the landlord must follow when a tenant fails to pay rent or violates any terms of the lease agreement. The landlord must give the tenant *written notice* of the violation and provide three days in which the tenant can remedy the problem. If at all possible the notice must be delivered personally. If personal delivery is not possible because the tenant is absent from his or her place of residence and usual place of business, then a copy of the notice may be left with a person of suitable age and discretion either at the tenant's residence or place of business. In that case a copy of the notice must be mailed, addressed to the tenant at his or her place of residence. If the above requirements cannot be fulfilled, the following steps must be taken:

1.   A copy of the notice must be posted in a conspicuous place on the property.

2.   If a person residing on the premises can be found, a copy must be left with that person.

3.   A copy must be mailed to the tenant at the address where the property is situated.

If the tenant does not remedy the violation the landlord *cannot use force*. The next step would be to institute formal legal proceedings. The advice of an attorney should be sought.

When the landlord pursues formal legal eviction *solely for the purpose of evicting a tenant due to non-payment of rent*, the legal proceedings are referred to as a *quick eviction*. The trial *must* be held within 12 days after the lawsuit is filed with the court, unless the landlord requests a later date. The tenant must be given written notice of the action by being served with a copy of the summons and the complaint at least five days prior to the court hearing. The tenant can request a continuance, but only for two days, unless the tenant deposits with the clerk of the court a security deposit such as a sum of money equal to the rent due and owing.

IF THE LANDLORD IS BRINGING AN ACTION FOR A BREACH OF THE LEASE OTHER THAN NONPAYMENT OF RENT, THE QUICK EVICTION PROVISION DOES NOT APPLY.

When the landlord is successful, the court judgment will be for restitution of the premises to the landlord and also may include the landlord's court costs and disbursements. If the property is five acres or less in size, the judgment may be enforced immediately. The sheriff is directed to remove the tenant and all of the tenant's possessions from the property and return the property to the landlord. If the property is larger than five acres in size, the judgment is delayed for five days. During this five-day period and the tenant has not reinstated the lease, the judgment will be enforced and the tenant and his or her possessions can be removed.

In situations where the landlord not only brings action for possession but also brings action for other breaches, such as damages or rent, the judgment handed down by the court also may direct the sheriff to levy the tenant's property to satisfy the judgment. The amount of the judgment established by the court usually equals the amount of the unpaid rent or damage. However, the court may require the tenant to pay three times the amount of damages suffered along with court costs and the fees of the landlord's attorney.

Tenant's Remedies

The landlord is obligated to provide reasonable waterproofing and water protection; to provide premises that are free of hazard to the health and safety of the tenant; and to maintain in good working order electrical, plumbing, heating, ventilating, cooling or sanitary facilities that are provided. If necessary the tenant can resort to court action to get the landlord to provide these services. Idaho law has not been established as to whether the tenant has a legal right to withhold rent and/or to complete the repairs and then seek reimbursement from the landlord. Such rights apparently *do not exist*.

If the tenant's intent is to require the landlord to provide the necessary services the tenant must give the landlord *written notice*, listing each violation and demanding that the violations be cured. This written notice must be delivered to the landlord or the landlord's agent personally, be mailed to the landlord or agent by certified mail with return receipt requested, or, if the landlord or agent is absent from the place of business, be left with an employee at the usual place of business.

The landlord must be given three days in which to cure the violations. The tenant can institute formal legal proceedings to require the landlord to cure the violations if the landlord has not complied with the request. The court action has the same early trial provisions that the landlord has when suit is brought for possession. The trial must be held within 12 days after the lawsuit is filed with the court, unless the tenant requests a later date. The landlord must be given written notice of the action by being served with a copy of the summons and the complaint at least five days prior to the court hearing.

If the tenant prevails, the judge will order the landlord to fulfill the obligations and may order the landlord to pay the court costs and the fees of the tenant's attorney. The tenant also may bring formal legal proceedings to recover money damages, if the tenant has lost money or otherwise been injured as a result of the landlord's failure. If the tenant prevails in this situation, the court has the authority to require the landlord to pay three times the amount of the tenant's damages.

THE MOBILE HOME PARK LANDLORD-TENANT ACT OF 1980

The Mobile Home Park Landlord-Tenant Act of 1980 formally established a set of specific rights and responsibilities for both the mobile home park owners and mobile home park tenants. Those situations not specifically covered under the 1980 act are covered by the general provisions of the landlord-tenant laws.

Written Lease Agreement

With limited exceptions the 1980 act requires the mobile home lot owner to provide a written lease agreement upon request. Either the landlord or the tenant may require the written agreement. This lease agreement must include:

1.   payment terms, including the time and place of payment,

2.   park rules,

3.   the name and address of the manager of the mobile home park,

4.   the name and address of the owner of the mobile home park or the name and address of an agent of the owner who resides within the county where the mobile home park is located, and

5.   the terms and conditions under which a security deposit may be withheld by the landlord upon termination of the lease agreement.

The lease agreement cannot provide for an entrance fee or an exit fee, nor can it require or permit a tenant to waive any rights or remedies provided by the 1980 act.

Park Rules

The mobile home park rules are enforceable only if they have been made part of the lease agreement signed by the tenant. Changes in the park rules can be made not more than four times annually. Any changes become effective upon the consent of the tenant, upon 90 days' notice to tenants with children or pets and upon 60 days' notice to all other tenants.

Rent Increases

The lease agreement may provide for rent increases (or decreases) upon 30 days' written notice. This 30-day provision applies only for the increases or decreases from ad valorem taxes, utility assessments or other service fees included in the monthly rent. All other rent increases require 90 days' written notice to the tenant.

Renewal and Termination

All lease agreements are automatically renewed unless the landlord gives the tenant at least 90 days' written notice of intent not to renew the lease agreement or the tenant gives 30 days' written notice of intent not to renew the lease agreement. A tenant may terminate upon 30 days' written notice if employment requires a change in residence and upon less than 30 days' notice if reassignment with the armed forces does not allow longer notice. The landlord may terminate the lease agreement during the term of the lease under the following conditions:

1. if tenant does not pay rent or other charges provided for in the lease agreement, or

2. if tenant substantially or repeatedly violates the mobile home park rules.

In either case the landlord must give the tenant three days to comply by paying the rent or charges owed or by remedying the violations. If the tenant does not comply at the end of three days, the tenant may be given 20 days in which to vacate the mobile home park.

Security Deposits

Security deposits for mobile homes are governed by the general landlord-tenant law, except that the mobile home park landlord must maintain a separate record of deposits.

Liability of the Lienholder or Legal Owner of a Mobile Home for Back Rent and Utilities

Idaho law does *not* specifically provide for the creation of a lien on the mobile home on behalf of a mobile home park owner for unpaid rent and utilities. Any lienholder or legal owner of a mobile home is required by Idaho law to notify the mobile home park owner, in writing, of any secured or legal interest in the mobile home. If the tenant falls 60 days behind in rent or appears to have abandoned the mobile home, the mobile home park landlord must notify the lienholder or legal owner of responsibility for any costs accruing for the mobile home space. The lienholder or legal owner shall be held responsible for utilities from the date of the notice. In addition, the lienholder or legal owner is also responsible for the rent due, including the past rent up to a maximum of 60 days prior to the date of notice.

Before the mobile home may be removed form the mobile home space, a signed written agreement from the mobile home park landlord, owner or manager must be received giving clearance for removal. This clearance normally will not be obtained until all monies due have been paid in full or a written agreement has been reached between the legal owner and the landlord of the mobile home park.

Sale of Mobile Home

Any mobile home owner has the right to sell his or her mobile home. If the mobile home lot owner helps the mobile home owner sell the mobile home, a commission can be paid. For the commission to be paid, a written agreement voluntarily entered into by the mobile home owner must have been completed. The mobile home park owner may require 30 days' written notice prior to the sale if the purchaser of the mobile home intends to leave the mobile home in the park. A new lease agreement must be signed by the park owner and the prospective tenant prior to the sale of the mobile home.

Rights and Remedies

A mobile home park owner may not take any action as retaliation because the tenant has exercised legal rights such as complaining about maintenance or the safety conditions of the park or becoming a member of a tenant's organization. The landlord cannot retaliate by terminating the lease, refusing to renew a lease, increasing rent or decreasing services.

The tenant is protected because of a breach by the landlord under the general landlord-tenant laws. Under the mobile home laws, the tenant is required to file an indemnity bond or monies to cover the landlord's legal expenses and court costs. If the tenant is not awarded damages or specific performance, the landlord will be reimbursed for legal expenses and court costs from the bond or monies.

OIL AND GAS LEASES

When oil and gas exploration companies negotiate to lease land to explore for oil and gas, a special lease agreement must be negotiated. A cash payment is usually paid to the landlord when the lease agreement is executed. If no well is drilled within a year or the stated period in the lease, the lease expires. Most oil and gas leases provide for the payment of another flat rental to continue its rights for another year. This type of payment may be paid annually until a well is produced. When a producing well is found, the landlord usually receives one-eighth of the production (or the value of that amount of production) as a royalty. The lease continues as long as oil or gas is obtained in significant quantities.

DISCRIMINATION

It is against both state and federal laws to have terms in a lease agreement that would violate fair housing laws. Care must also be taken in the way tenants are selected and treated to ensure that both federal and state laws are not violated.

QUESTIONS

1. Melinda Jones leases an apartment on a weekly basis with rent of $55 per week. No specific termination date is shown on the written lease agreement. Jones has been informed by her boss that she is being transferred to another state and must be at her new office within three weeks. Under Idaho law, how much notice must she give the landlord in order to terminate the lease agreement?

   a. One week
   b. 90 days
   c. 30 days
   d. Five days

2. The Idaho Statute of Frauds requires a lease to be in writing if it is for a term of more than:

   a. six months.
   b. one year.
   c. five years.
   d. Anytime

3. Under the usual oil and gas lease, the property owner receives a:

   a. set monthly rental, whether or not oil or gas is obtained from the land.
   b. separate fee for every well that is drilled.
   c. yearly fee for the use of the property, plus an additional fee to be negotiated if and when oil or gas is obtained from the property.
   d. yearly fee for the use of the property plus a stated percentage of the production of the oil and gas as a royalty.

4. A landlord probably has the right to enter the property, without permission to inspect, if:

   a. the landlord has reasonable cause to believe that damage is occurring to the property.
   b. a tenant is in default in rent and has been absent from the premises for a considerable period of time.
   c. All of the above
   d. None of the above

5. If the landlord plans on a rent increase, a written notice must be given to the tenant at least how many days before the end of the term and prior to the date if the increase is to become effective on all periodic tenancies?

   a. 30 days
   b. 15 days
   c. No notice required
   d. Seven days

6. If a tenant leaves property of value behind after vacating the premises, how must a landlord legally dispose of the property?

   a. Dispose of it immediately.
   b. Follow abandoned or unclaimed property laws.
   c. Store it until tenant returns.
   d. Safeguard it.

7. The landlord is obligated to provide:

   a. reasonable waterproofing and water protection.
   b. premises that are not hazardous to the health and safety of the tenant.
   c. electrical, plumbing, heating, ventilating, cooling or sanitary facilities in good working order.
   d. All of the above

8. A security deposit can be used for all of the following *except*:

   a. rent.
   b. pets.
   c. negligent abuse of the premises.
   d. careless misuse of the landlord's contents.

9. When a property is more than five acres in size and the landlord is successful in the court judgment for restitution of the premises, the maximum length of time from the date of notice of default to repossession of the property will be:

   a. 22 days.
   b. 17 days.
   c. 20 days.
   d. Cannot determine from information given

10. The Mobile Home Park Landlord-Tenant Act was passed in what year?

    a. 1970
    b. 1980
    c. 1985
    d. 1975

18

Real Estate Appraisal

MARKET VALUE

Chapter 18 in the text discusses real estate appraisal from the professional real estate appraiser's point of view. This supplementary chapter, in contrast, will deal with the role of the real estate salesperson in determining a property's fair market value at the time of listing, a subject touched upon in Chapter 5 of the text.

When professional real estate appraisers determine the value of a property they use one or all of the three approaches to value, depending on the type of property being valued. As discussed in the text, the three approaches to estimating real estate values are:

1. *Cost Approach*, determined by computing the cost of reproducing the physical property, less depreciation, plus the value of the land

2. *Income Approach*, figured by determining the income (either net operating income or gross income) and the appropriate capitalization rate or gross multiplier

3. *Market Approach*, an estimate of value based on comparison with other properties that have recently sold.

In contrast to these approaches, a real estate sales associate will do a competitive market analysis. How the real estate sales associate prepares and uses the competitive market analysis often will determine whether the property is listed at the correct price or a listing is obtained at all. The appraisal process to determine value is not an exact science that can predict an exact sales price. Using the competitive market analysis approach, the real estate sales associate can predict a reasonable range of values. The limitation faced by a real estate appraiser actually turns out to be an advantage for the sales associate. By preparing a range of prices, the owner will be prepared for an offer anywhere in that range.

COMPETITIVE MARKET ANALYSIS

To adequately prepare a competitive market analysis, the sales associate will need to gather as much information as possible, as discussed in the following sections.

Market Data

1. In gathering market information, a sales associate will attempt to find as many comparable sales as possible. These sales should be recent (three to six months) actual sales of comparable properties in the area.

2. Information also will be gathered about currently listed properties, which the subject property will have to compete with. The current competitive properties will tend to set the upper end of the value range.

3. Additional market information will be gathered about properties that were listed, did not sell and are no longer on the market. These will help show the seller consequences of not listing the property at a realistic price.

4. A sales associate also should gather information that may be available from any FHA or VA appraisals that may have been done on comparable properties.

A broker's listings and/or MLS files are a prime source for researching these facts. *Note that the more comparable the properties a sales associate selects for use in the analysis, the more accurate the market comparison will be.* It is also important to make sure that all the facts are totally accurate. Many standard competitive market analysis forms are available for use in presenting market data to a seller.

Other Listing Information

Location. The location of the property will have a major impact on the listed price. A property located in a fine neighborhood, close to schools and shopping, and with light traffic will usually sell at a higher price. The location, along with highly valued extras such as landscaping, view, covered patio, fireplace and the like will add to the buyer appeal. This buyer appeal equates to a higher selling price.

Energy-Saving Features

The number and types of energy-saving features as well as the amount of money saved will have a significant impact on the buyer. If the savings are large enough, the buyer will be willing to pay more for the property.

Motivation. The seller's reason for moving and his or her needs and emotional makeup will determine how the property is priced. The level of motivation will affect the seller's reaction to offers for sale.

If the seller has bought a new home that will not be ready for five months and thinks the market value of properties is going up by $5,000 during that time, he or she may set the sales price much higher than the competition. Salespersons should be prepared to discuss the possible consequences of these actions.

People who change homes frequently to take new assignments often have a realistic view of pricing a house. Some sellers may choose to carry a house vacant for several months before becoming realistic. Others feel overextended and want to "get out from under." These are the kinds of motivators a salesperson must know about to list the property.

Terms of financing. What financing is available? Are conventional loans, FHA or VA loans available and what will be the cost to the seller? Can the buyer assume the seller's existing mortgage? Will the seller help finance by accepting a second mortgage, contract for deed, or a low down payment? Answers to these questions will help determine the pricing strategy and the final listing price.

Drawbacks. Needless to say, a property's drawbacks can reduce its market value dramatically. Certain construction flaws (a bad floor plan, small rooms or low ceilings in the basement) cannot be corrected readily and may have to be left as is. Minor drawbacks, (poor maintenance, leaky plumbing or cracked plaster), can be repaired. By pointing out repairable drawbacks in the listing presentation and demonstrating the negative effects they can have on the property's market value, the sales associate may be able to persuade the seller to correct them.

THE FINAL LISTING PRICE

After all necessary information has been gathered and is ready to present to the seller, the sales associate should be able to get the seller to list the property at a marketable price. After the final sales price range has been determined, the final listing price can be determined.

Importance of an Appropriate Listing Price

Overpriced listings seldom sell. They create bad relations with the owner and harm the brokerage firm's reputation. Listings that expire unsold create an image of failure and eventually decrease your ability to obtain quality listings in your area. The larger the number of marginal listings you take, the lower your chances of success.

QUESTIONS

1. What method of market analysis is generally used by a real estate sales associate or broker when preparing to establish the listing price?

   a. Cost approach
   b. Market data approach
   c. Income approach
   d. Competitive market analysis approach

2. Sources for the market data analysis include:

   a. FHA appraisals.
   b. brokerage listing records.
   c. MLS files.
   d. All of the above

3. The final listing price will be affected by:

   a. location.
   b. appeal.
   c. seller's motivation.
   d. All of the above

19

Land-Use Controls

IDAHO LOCAL LAND USE PLANNING ACT OF 1975

The Local Planning Act (Idaho Code 67-6501 to 67-6529) repealed the former planning and zoning authority (I.C. Title 50, Chapters 11 and 12) of cities and the former zoning authority of counties (I.C. Title 31, Chapter 38). With the enactment of the Local Planning Act, the Idaho legislature prescribed, in much greater detail, the terms and conditions for exercising regulatory authority over land use. A fundamental requirement is that the adoption of a comprehensive plan is a prerequisite to exercising zoning and subdivision control. Beyond this planning requirement, the act established basic standards and procedures that local governments must follow in order to establish and administer a system of land-use controls.

Standards and procedures contained in the act fall into three categories:

1. requirements for the organizational framework to enact and administer land-use regulations,

2. requirements for establishing and amending regulatory measures (the plan, the zoning ordinance, the subdivision ordinance), and

3. requirements for administration of permits under adopted regulatory measures (special uses, planned unit developments, subdivision approvals and variances).

THE ORGANIZATIONAL FRAMEWORK OF THE LOCAL PLANNING ACT

The Local Planning Act permits local governments to enjoy considerable leeway in establishing an organizational framework for regulating land use. The governing board (the city council or county commissioners) may exercise authority directly; delegate all or part of its authority (except for the authority to enact ordinances) to a planning commission and a zoning commission or a combined planning and zoning commission; or provide for initial decisions by a commission with appeal to the governing board. Governing boards in the affected jurisdictions also may establish joint planning, zoning or planning and zoning commissions. Also, ordinances may provide for the appointment of hearing examiners to hear and make recommendations concerning particular permit applications.

Membership on commissions may range from three to 12 persons who have resided in the county at least five years. On county commissions, two-thirds of the membership must reside in unincorporated areas. Membership may exceed 12 if necessary to achieve proportional representation on city commissions operating under impact area agreements or on joint planning commissions. The commissions are required to adopt bylaws, hold regular meetings at least once a month for nine months of the year and maintain records of meetings and other actions taken.

Members of governing boards and commissions are prohibited from acting in any case where the member or a person with an employment, business or family relationship with a member, has an economic interest. Members are required to reveal any conflict or potential conflict before the matter is considered.

THE COMPREHENSIVE PLAN

In contrast to the rather ambiguous role of planning in land-use regulation in the past, the Local Planning Act requires:

1.   preparation and adoption of a plan document,

2.   zoning to be in accordance with the adopted plan, and

3.   plan amendment before any rezone request is approved that is inconsistent with the plan.

The Local Planning Act requires local governments to adopt a plan covering historical and existing conditions, trends and future goals and objectives for eleven specified elements, unless an explanation is given why a particular element is unnecessary. The specificity required for each of these elements varies.

The apparent purpose in giving the plan greater than advisory effect is to require communities to articulate the policies they will pursue in exercising land-use controls so that interested persons are given notice of what to expect.

Adoption, Amendment or Repeal of Comprehensive Plan

The Local Planning Act requires the following for the adoption, amendment or repeal of the comprehensive plan:

1.   two-stage notice and hearing process before planning (or planning and zoning) commission and governing board,

2.   republication of notice and additional hearing at either the commission or governing board level if "material changes" are made after a public hearing,

3.   adoption by governing board via "resolution or ordinance,"

4.   publication of plan (may be by reference), and

5.   special provisions applying to plan amendment:

    a.   standard: to correct "errors in the original plan or to recognize substantial changes in the actual condition of the area," and

    b.   frequency of changes:

        1)   any person may petition for a plan change at any time, and

        2)   the commission may recommend amendments to the plan not more often than once every six months.

THE ZONING ORDINANCE

Historically, the use of private land in this country has been regulated by local units of government. Even today, with state and federal governments playing an increasing role in land-use regulation, local governments retain the principal mechanisms for regulating land use. Of all the different powers local governments have to control the use and development of land, including regulatory authority (zoning, subdivision ordinances and building codes), budgetary power (such as investments in water and sewer facilities and services and eminent domain) and taxing authority, *zoning* constitutes the most fundamental and far-reaching power.

Zoning authority consists of the power to regulate, for all legitimate police power purposes, the location and intensity of various uses of land as well as the power to regulate the physical design and arrangement of structures on land. Thus zoning ordinances, which prescribe standards for development and building design, may overlap areas covered by building, subdivision or other ordinances. However, the central and distinctive feature of zoning is the power to define different types and intensities of *uses* and to prescribe their location within a particular jurisdiction by means of mapped districts.

Regulatory Standards

The heart of a typical zoning ordinance is the sections setting forth different types and intensities of uses and the standards that apply to each. A typical zoning ordinance will recognize at least four major uses: residential, commercial, industrial and agricultural. The agricultural category may represent an active use category, designed to conserve agricultural land and prevent conflict with agricultural operations, or it may represent a holding category designed to be rezoned according to its highest and best use when the market creates a demand for its development. Ordinarily, these major uses will be further subdivided into additional districts that represent different densities or types and intensities of these uses. Thus, residential use may be subdivided into high, medium and low density and/or be categorized by different housing types (single family, multiple family, mobile homes and such).

In any event, uses predating new zoning restrictions must be allowed to continue as nonconforming uses, although they ordinarily will be restricted from expansion and may be subject to termination over a period of time.

Within the text of the ordinance setting forth the different use zones (or in a separate district designed to be superimposed over the use districts), standards for building design and arrangements of structures are specified. These regulations typically include height, yard, setback and parking requirements and may include a variety of other design and performance standards.

Within any use district, allowable types of use are set forth. These uses fall into one of two categories:

1. "permitted" uses (permitted as a matter of right, as long as the various design requirements are observed), and

2. "special" or "conditional" uses (can be permitted by the commission or governing board if such uses are determined to meet special design and performance standards and are compatible with neighboring uses).

Administrative Procedures

Usually the latter portions of a zoning ordinance are devoted to administrative procedures. In this portion the office authorized to pass on disputed interpretations of ordinances, to act on variances, special-use and other permits, and requests for rezoning are designated. Also, the procedures for dealing with each are set forth. Included in this portion of the ordinance are any general standards that apply to permits and rezone requests. Steps must be taken to ensure that ordinance procedures follow minimum requirements established for various decisions by state statutes and that the prescribed procedures are adhered to in handling specific requests.

Adoption, Amendment or Repeal of Zoning Ordinance

The Local Land Use Planning Act requires the following actions for the adoption, amendment or repeal of zoning ordinances:

1. two-stage notice and hearing process before zoning (or planning and zoning) commission and governing board,

2. publication pursuant to I.C. 50-907 and I.C. 37-715, and

3. special provisions concerning amendment or ordinance:

    a. If a boundary change (presumably any map amendment) is involved, *notice by mail* must be made on all landowners within the land being considered and all landowners "impacted" (as determined by the commission) by the proposed change.

    b. If the proposed amendment is inconsistent with the plan, an amendment of the plan must be adopted (by means of the two-stage notice and hearing process) before the ordinance is amended.

Standards and Procedures for Administration of Permits

General requirements for issuance of all permits under the Local Planning Act (special-use permits, planned unit development (PUD) permits, variance permits and subdivision permits) are:

1. Standards:

    a. Procedures for processing all permits for which a fee is charged must be set forth in the zoning, subdivision or other ordinance.

    b. Rules must be adopted by the governing board establishing a time period for action by the commission and the board for all permits.

2. Procedure:

    a. All permits must be referred to the zoning (or planning and zoning) commission for recommendation and can be assigned to the commission for decision.

    b. The grant or denial of a permit must specify the following:

        1) ordinance or standards used

    2)   reasons for the action, and

    3)   actions, if any, the applicant could take to obtain a permit.

Beyond the requirements of this section, the act contains different minimum standards and procedures for the different types of permits. These standards and procedures are covered in detail in the following sections of the act:

1. special provisions applying to special-use permits (I.C. 67-6512) and PUD permits (I.C. 67-6515),

2. special provisions applying to variance permits (I.C. 67-6516),

3. special provisions having principal application to variance and subdivision permits (I.C. 67-6521), and

4. special provisions relating to subdivisions (not part of Title 67, Local Planning Act).

SUBDIVISION CONTROLS

Subdivision regulations are intended to protect the local community from the creation and development of poorly designed and ill-equipped neighborhoods. The regulations require that new streets be properly constructed and logically related to the existing street system with which they connect; that newly developed land be provided with basic services; that other residents be protected from the financial impact of initial installation costs; that the subdivision be consistent with zoning regulations; and, sometimes, that the owners and developers of the subdivision bear the cost of providing open space necessary to serve the recreational and environmental needs of the future inhabitants of the subdivision. The broad purpose of subdivision controls is to *guide* community development and to protect prospective residents and neighboring owners from the evils of poorly designed areas.

Regulation of the subdivision of land for the protection of the public health, safety and welfare are within, and constitute a valid exercise of, the police powers delegated to cities and counties. In Idaho reasonable subdivision regulations have been upheld under the constitutional grant of police powers, even without enabling legislation. By statute, however, cities and counties now are *required* to provide standards for subdivision permits.

By statute a subdivision is defined as a tract of land divided into five or more lots, parcels or sites for the purpose of sale or building development, whether immediate or future, except for agricultural purposes.

Cities (but not counties) have the power to approve or disapprove subdivision plats within one mile of their corporate boundaries and, by agreement between an individual city and county, the city may be authorized to extend its subdivision regulations even further into the unincorporated areas of the county. Counties have no authority to exercise their subdivision controls within incorporated cities although, through use of a joint service agreement, a city presumably could contract with a county to have the county's officers enforce the city's subdivision ordinances within the city. Sewer and water facilities provided to a subdivision must be approved by the Idaho State Department of Health and Welfare (if the subdivision exceeds 25 lots) or the local health district before the subdivision plat may be recorded.

Typically the local subdivision ordinances contain standards for street width and construction; continuity with existing streets; installation of paving, curbs, gutters and sidewalks; drainage facilities, provision of water and sewer facilities, including easements thereto; and dedication of required rights-of-way. Such ordinances usually provide that no subdivision plat may be recorded, nor may any sales of lots or blocks within a subdivision occur until provision has been made for the installation, immediately or in the future, of the required dedication and improvements. Because the county recorder cannot accept a plat for filing without proof of the required approvals, subdivision regulations must be met before a subdivider may record the plat and sell the lots and blocks within the subdivision.

Subdivision standards may be included as part of the subdivision ordinance itself, or as part of a zoning or planned unit development ordinance, or they may be set forth by a separate ordinance. Procedural requirements for adoption of subdivision ordinances are the same as for the adoption of comprehensive plans and zoning ordinances. Hearings before the planning, or planning and zoning, commission and the governing body are required for adoption or amendment. Existing subdivision ordinances may be updated and amended in the same manner.

At the heart of modern subdivision ordinances is the requirement of *dedication* of property within the subdivision for public use, such as streets, alleys, drainage, sewers, water lines and sometimes (especially under the more recent subdivision ordinances) for parks and even schools or other public facilities. Dedication is a conveyance of an interest in land to the government for a public purpose. A dedication of land has an important affect on the subdivider, the public and purchasers of land in the subdivision. In affect, the subdivider parts with ownership, even where the dedication is only an easement. The public obtains the dedicated land without cost. The purchaser will be assured proper access and utilities but probably will pay more for the land than otherwise would be the case.

Under Idaho law the owner of land included in a subdivision plat must make a dedication, on the plat, of all the streets and alleys shown on the plat. Local ordinances usually require additional dedication for utility easements. The effect of acknowledging and recording the plat is equivalent to a deed in fee simple of such portion of the premises platted as is on such plat set apart for streets or other public use. However, no street or alley so dedicated shall be deemed a public street or alley until the dedication is accepted and confirmed by the governing body of the city or county.

BUILDING, HOUSING, PLUMBING, FIRE, ELECTRICAL AND GAS CODES

Police power enables cities and counties, in the interest of public safety, to enact codes governing building and housing construction, fire prevention and the installation of plumbing, electrical and gas distribution systems and fixtures. Early Idaho Supreme Court cases upheld the power of cities to enact and enforce fire and building codes. Idaho statutes also recognize local governmental authority in this area. The Idaho legislature has expressly declared building codes to be within the public health, safety and welfare.

One common method by which local governments regulate construction of buildings is by adoption of the Uniform Building Code (UBC) published by the International Conference of Building Officials. Idaho statutes specifically authorize cities and counties to adopt such codes by ordinance without publishing the entire code. In addition the Idaho legislature has adopted the Uniform Building Code and other nationally recognized codes and has made them applicable (with certain exceptions, including farms) throughout the state. Local governments are required to comply with each code and may provide inspection and enforcement, or may leave the inspection and enforcement duties to the State Department of Labor and Industrial Services.

The purpose of the UBC is to provide minimum standards to safeguard life or limb, health, property and public welfare by regulating and controlling the design, construction, quality of materials, use and occupancy, location and maintenance of all buildings and structures and certain equipment in them. The

UBC and its related codes, such as the Housing Code, Mechanical Code, Uniform Code on Abatement of Dangerous Buildings and others, must be constructed in conjunction with local zoning ordinances.

A related, nationally recognized code is the Uniform Fire Code, published jointly by the International Conference of Building Officials and the Western Fire Chiefs Association. The intent of the Uniform Fire Code is to prescribe regulations for safeguarding life and property from the hazards of fire and explosion arising from the storage, handling and use of hazardous substances, materials and devices and from conditions hazardous to life or property in the use or occupancy of buildings or premises. The code contains specific regulations on explosives, gases, lumberyards, building exits and the like.

Additional fire and life safety regulations are contained in the Life Safety Code, published by the National Fire Protection Association. The provisions of this code overlap to some extent with the Uniform Fire Code. A local government that adopts both codes must specify in the adopting ordinance which code will prevail where overlap occurs.

Nationally recognized codes on plumbing, electrical and gas installation are also adopted by local governments in Idaho. All of these codes are directed at promoting public safety and must be used for that purpose. The codes are not intended as devices to prevent growth but are important and necessary growth guidance tools in that they require a certain quality of growth by specifying minimum construction and safety standards.

ANNEXATION

Idaho law permits cities, in certain circumstances, to expand their boundaries by annexing adjacent property. This power is statutory, is not inherent in cities and is not a part of a city's police power. Although county boundaries also may be altered, subject to certain constitutional provisions, and although some special districts also have annexation powers, the focus of this section is on the power of cities to annex adjacent unincorporated territory into the corporate limits, with or without the approval of the county or of the owners of the property. This is a *unilateral* power in that, as long as the requirements set forth by statute are met, Idaho cities may enlarge their boundaries merely by passing the proper ordinance, without the prior consent of anyone other than the city council.

The statutory requirements for annexation of unincorporated territory by cities are set forth in Idaho Code Section 50-222. The first requirement is that the land to be annexed must be *contiguous* or *adjacent* to the city. The terms *contiguous* and *adjacent* have been defined in a number of Idaho Supreme Court decisions; the later cases have tended to strictly explain the requirement as meaning that the property to be annexed must be physically adjacent to or abutting the city.

After the requirement of contiguity is met, the area may be annexed if any one of the following conditions exists:

1. The property has been, by the owner or by any person with the owner's authority or acquiescence, laid off into blocks containing not more than five acres of land each, whether platted or not.

2. The owner or proprietor or any person by or with the owner's authority has sold or begun to sell off such lands in tracts not exceeding five acres.

3. The owner or proprietor or any person by or with the owner's authority requests annexation in writing to the council.

4.   The tract is entirely surrounded by properties lying within the city boundaries.

The courts have construed the statute to mean that after a single sale has occurred from a tract of five acres or less, whether subdivided and platted or not, then the *entire tract* may be annexed, even though the remainder is more than five acres. Even the acts of prior owners of the property may subject the land to annexation, although the court has held that, if the tract is presently larger than five acres and the *present* owner has not subdivided or begun to sell in tracts of five acres or less, the burden of proof is on the city to show that some property in question was in his or her ownership.

There is an additional limitation on a city's power to annex. Idaho Code provides that a city may annex "only those areas which can be reasonably assumed to be used for orderly development of the city." Assuming that the annexation ordinance has been enacted validly, certain additional procedural requirements must be observed. First the city must comply with Idaho Code by filing certified copies of the annexation ordinance, legal description and map with the appropriate county offices and with State Tax Commission. Second, following the procedures set forth in the Local Planning Act, the city must provide for the zoning designation of the annexed area. Zoning must take place simultaneously with the annexation because the Idaho Code provides: "Concurrently or immediately following the adoption of an ordinance of annexation, the city council must amend the comprehensive plan and zoning ordinance."

An important limitation on cities' annexation powers is the Idaho Code provision that permits agricultural lands, whether platted or unplatted, to be detached from a city through proceedings in district court. The requirements for such detachment of agricultural lands are fairly simple and, if an owner can show that all requirements are met, the owner has a legal right to de-annexation from the city, regardless of the effect on the city's comprehensive planning process.

For agricultural de-annexation to occur, the following requirements must be met:

1.   The property must contain not fewer than five acres.

2.   The property must be within the corporate limits of a city.

3.   The property must be used exclusively for agricultural purposes. (The existence of a railroad or canal on the property does not amount to a nonagricultural purpose.)

4.   The property does not receive sufficient special benefits to justify its retention in the city.

5.   By detachment of the lands, the symmetry of the city would not be materially marred.

SPECIAL DISTRICTS

Numerous special districts may be created in Idaho to provide particular services to residents and owners of property. These include such special districts as auditorium, cemetery, drainage, fire protection, flood control, highway (including the old "good road" districts), hospital, irrigation, library, mosquito abatement, port, recreation, school, sewer, soil conservation, water, combined water and sewer, and watershed improvement districts, as well as city-created or county-created authorities, urban renewal agencies, housing authorities and regional airport authorities.

Special districts differ from "general" governmental entities primarily in that special districts have no general governmental powers. They usually provide only a single, special governmental service. Special districts do not have the authority to pass general regulatory ordinances or to provide other governmental services beyond those specifically set forth in their enabling legislation.

QUESTIONS

1. The fundamental requirement of the Idaho Local Land Use Planning Act of 1975 is the adoption of a:

   a. zoning ordinance.
   b. comprehensive plan.
   c. subdivision ordinance.
   d. All of the above

2. Any land use in existence prior to the adoption of a new zoning restriction must be allowed to continue as a:

   a. conditional use.
   b. special use.
   c. nonconforming use.
   d. variance.

3. Any amendment or repeal of a zoning ordinance or change in a zoning boundary requires notice by mail to be made to all landowners who are:

   a. impacted.
   b. of legal voting age.
   c. both a and b.
   d. Not required to notify

4. By statute, a subdivision is defined as a tract of land divided into _____ or _____ lots, parcels or sites for the purpose of sale, building or development, whether immediate or future, except for agricultural purposes.

   a. four . . . more
   b. five . . . fewer
   c. five . . . more
   d. six . . . more

5. Cities (but not counties) have the power to approve or disapprove subdivision plats within how many miles of their corporate boundaries?

   a. One-half mile
   b. One mile
   c. Two miles
   d. Do not have this power

6. Sewer and water facilities provided to a subdivision must be approved by the Idaho State Department of Health and Welfare if the number of subdivision lots exceeds

   a. ten.   c. 100.
   b. 50.   d. 25.

7. All but which of the following fall within a city's police powers?

   a. Zoning ordinances
   b. Annexation
   c. Building codes
   d. Fire codes

8. Buildings or improvements that are in existence prior to the adoption of a new zoning ordinance may be classified as:

   a. conditional uses.
   b. special uses.
   c. nonconforming structures.
   d. variances.

Idaho Fair Housing

DISCRIMINATION IN HOUSING

Many states or municipalities adopt fair housing laws. The Idaho legislature has not adopted any changes in the Idaho Code to reflect the new federal fair housing laws enacted on March 12, 1989, by the federal government. Idaho's Fair Housing Law already included minimal protection of handicapped individuals. Even though the Idaho law does not include the new protected classes of familial status and handicapped in their law, the federal fair housing laws would directly apply.

The Idaho Fair Housing Law prohibits discrimination in housing based on race, creed, color, religion, sex, handicap, national origin or ancestry. *Discrimination based on any of these factors is prohibited in the following business transactions:*

1. *Refusing to show, rent, lease, sell or transfer housing.* Housing includes apartments, condominiums, duplexes and similar attached housing, mobile homes and trailer courts, vacant lands, commercial property and private homes. The only exemption is a room for rent in a home occupied by the owner or renter.

   Example: John was told that the house he wanted to rent was no longer available but he still sees the For Rent sign up the next day.

2. *Causing unequal terms, conditions and privileges of housing*

   Example: Sue calls on a duplex and is quoted terms of $400 per month. When she talks to the other tenants she finds that all of the men in the complex pay only $325 per month.

3. *Causing unequal terms, conditions and privileges in obtaining and using financial assistance for the purchase, construction or maintenance of housing*

   Example: Melinda, a single, divorced female, was required to pay for a credit report and have her father cosign the loan. After talking to a male friend, she learns that he was not required to have a cosigner or pay for a credit report.

4. *Segregating and/or separating housing*

   Example: Jim makes arrangements with Ben Broker to look at houses for purchase or rent anywhere within the city. Ben Broker showed Jim houses in only one small select area of the city.

5. *Including or honoring discriminatory restrictive covenants*

Example: Your real estate agent indicates that the restrictive covenants of the subdivision would not allow you to purchase a home because you do not attend the right church.

6. *Advertising any discriminatory preference or limitation in housing, making any inquiry or reference that is discriminatory in nautre*

    Example: The owner indicates a policy against renting to you because you are single, divorced and have children, but you know others (a different sex, race or religion) who fall into these categories but have not been denied housing by the same owner.

7. *Aiding and abetting unfair housing practices, preventing any person from complying with fair housing practices*

    Example: Your real estate agent encourages you not to sell or rent to a person from a minority group.

8. *Retaliating against an employee or agent who complies with fair housing practices*

    Example: The real estate agent who helped you find a home was given less than the normal commission split and told to move his license to another office that handled clients of your ancestry.

9. *Refusing to receive and transmit any bona fide offer to buy, rent, sell or lease housing*

    Example: The real estate agent attempted to discourage you from making an offer and when you forced the issue, the agent did not present your offer to the seller.

In Idaho there is one exception in the area of discrimination: A religious institution or organization can give *preference* in a real estate transaction to members of the same religion.

The discrimination laws do not apply to rental of a:

1. room or rooms in a housing accommodation by an individual when that individual or a member of his or her family lives in the same housing accommodation, or

2. two-family dwelling (duplex) if the lessor or a member of the lessor's family lives in one of the units.

HOW TO FILE A CHARGE OF HOUSING DISCRIMINATION

If an individual believes he or she has been discriminated against, a charge of discrimination may be filed with:

1. Idaho Human Rights Commission
   450 West State Street
   Boise, Idaho 83720
   Phone: (208) 334-2873

2.   U.S. Department of Housing and Urban Development
Regional Office of Fair Housing
Arcade Plaza Building
1321 Second Avenue
Seattle, Washington 98101
Phone: (206) 442-4307

A charge must be filed with the Idaho Human Rights Commission within one year.

A charge must be filed with the U.S. Department of Housing and Urban Development (HUD) within 1 year, or sue upon in federal court within 2 years of the alleged act of discrimination.

WHAT HAPPENS WHEN A CHARGE IS FILED

The person charging discrimination will sign a formal complaint form that will allow the Human Rights Commission or HUD to investigate the case. Strict guidelines apply to the disclosure of information on a charge, and all information will remain confidential unless a case is authorized for hearing or court action. Most cases are resolved prior to reaching this stage.

A civil rights specialist will make every effort to settle the charge immediately, which often may result in a voluntary no-fault settlement. If a no-fault settlement does not occur, an investigation and interview will be conducted with all parties involved in the charge. If the facts do not support a finding of probable cause, the case will be dismissed. If the facts support the charge, a finding of probable cause will be made. Upon a finding of probable cause, attempts will be made to conciliate the case. If the conciliation is successful, the case will be closed with a settlement. If the conciliation effort is not successful, the case may be taken to a hearing or court action, or it may be dismissed.

The federal fair housing law has substantially changed the process of filing a complaint for discrimination with HUD. Also significantly changed are the penalties against an individual found guilty of discrimination. Refer to the main textbook or the latest HUD publication for information on the new federal fair housing law.

OTHER GROUPS CONCERNED WITH FAIR HOUSING

The Boise/Elmore Community Housing Resource Board was organized in March 1981 by HUD. The purpose of the board is to ensure equal opportunity in housing rental, sale or financing without regard to race, creed, color, religion, sex, national origin or ancestry in Ada and Elmore counties.

The Community Housing Resource Board will enforce equal opportunity in housing laws by:

• assessing the effectiveness of the Voluntary Affirmative Marketing Agreement, a program of voluntary compliance between HUD and the real estate industry in which REALTORS® voluntarily agree to promote equal housing opportunity,

• ensuring that no denial of equal professional service to individuals in the same housing market area occurs, and

• making the public aware of fair housing laws.

The two objectives of the Voluntary Affirmative Marketing Agreement are to maximize communication between the housing industry and protected classes within the community and to enhance opportunity for implementation of industry group commitments through initiation of projects and activities and effective evaluation and assessment of program progress.

QUESTIONS

1. The Idaho fair housing laws apply to:

    a. the rental of a room or rooms in a housing accommodation by an individual when that individual or a member of his or her family lives in the same housing accommodation.
    b. the rental of a two-family dwelling (duplex) if the lessor or a member of the lessor's family lives in one of the units.
    c. a religious institution or organization giving preference in a real estate transaction to members of the same religion.
    d. None of the above

2. Individuals who believe they have been discriminated against in rental of housing may file discrimination charges with the:

    a. Idaho Human Rights Commission.
    b. U.S. Department of Housing and Urban Development.
    c. Idaho Attorney General.
    d. Both a and b

3. A charge of housing discrimination must be filed with the Idaho Human Rights Commission within:

    a. one year.   c. 180 days.
    b. six months.   d. 270 days.

4. A charge of housing discrimination must be filed with the U.S. Department of Housing and Urban Development within:

    a. 180 days.
    b. 270 days.
    c. 1 year.
    d. No limit on time

23

Closing the Real Estate Transaction

THE CLOSING

In Idaho the majority of real estate sales transactions are closed in the office of the escrow closing agent, the financial institution or the broker. The listing or designated broker is responsible for the closing; however, one or both parties may desire an attorney to represent them and/or direct the closing. An independent and impartial escrow closing agent may handle the closing for a fee. Transactions that involve federally funded Farm Home Administration loans must be closed by either an attorney or a title company, as required by federal regulations.

Broker's Responsibility

In supervising the closing of a transaction, a broker must make sure that all necessary information is obtained, documents prepared and other details taken care of as provided by the terms of the purchase and sale agreement and/or earnest money agreement. Any deviation from these provisions should have the written consent of both buyer and seller.

In general the broker's responsibility in closing a transaction extends to every area that is listed on the closing statement or that otherwise affects ownership of the property being sold, including the following:

1. *Financial arrangements of both parties.* Preparations for any new financing, loan assumptions or loan payoffs must be coordinated by the broker so that any required mortgages, trust deeds, assignments, releases, contracts for deed or other papers are provided for and ready to be executed at the closing.

2. *Title considerations.* Items such as the seller's deed, the required evidence of title and any documents necessary to clear the seller's title must be obtained or prepared. In Idaho an abstract of title with an attorney's opinion or a title insurance policy is acceptable evidence of the seller's title; however, in recent years an owner's title insurance policy, furnished by the seller to the buyer, has been used almost exclusively.

When the buyer is financing the purchase through a lending institution, the lender will require an additional title insurance policy called a *mortgagee extended coverage policy,* which protects the lender's interest. The charge for this additional policy is customarily paid for by the buyer/borrower.

3. *Taxes and other liens, including mechanics' and energy liens and assessments of the Local Improvement District (LID).* Some of these must be paid off at the closing; others will have been paid in advance or will be due in the future.

4. *Public utility charges.* Final readings must be taken so that current bills can be prorated. Some utilities are paid in advance for the upcoming payment period, others are paid in arrears for the preceding payment period.

5. *Insurance.* Whether the buyer is taking out a new policy or taking over the seller's existing policy, arrangements for new coverage or assignment of existing coverage must be made in advance so a policy will be in effect at closing. When a buyer takes over a seller's policy, it is very important to get the buyer together with the seller's insurance agent before the closing because if the coverage on the seller is not adequate for the buyer and the buyer suffers a loss, the responsible broker may incur some liability.

Obtaining information and ordering documents. Closing statement information must be carefully prepared and documented. In preparing to close a real estate transaction the broker always must find the most reliable source for information—for example, the county assessor or treasurer for information concerning real estate taxes and the lending institution involved in the transaction for information on the current balance of an existing loan. The Idaho Code requires municipalities to record any LID lien with the county just like taxes and other liens. However, information regarding such assessments is apt to be more reliable when obtained from the clerk of the municipality where the payments are made instead of the county treasurer's office. Most public and private agencies will not accept liability for erroneous verbal information. The safest way is to get any loan payoffs, lien release amounts, irrigation company assessments and LID assessments in writing, dated and signed by the person giving the information.

What about the existing loan? Discovering whether the loan payments are up to date is not sufficient; the broker must know the date on which the interest is due in order to prorate that interest correctly. Many lenders require at least 30 days' prior notice when a loan is to be paid off or they can charge interest for an additional 30 days. If an existing loan is to be assumed by the buyer the lenders often require both buyer and seller to execute several different documents. It is very important to order an *assumption package* from the lender well in advance of the designated closing date. Often the lender charges for this service, payable in advance. The broker cannot be too careful in securing accurate information from reliable sources. A closing statement based on incorrect information can create problems and unnecessary expense for all concerned parties.

The same kind of care should be taken when the broker orders the preparation of deeds, installment sales contracts, escrow instructions, property insurance policies and title insurance policies. The accuracy of information supplied to the attorney, title company or other agency involved will determine the accuracy of the completed document.

Added care should be taken to ensure that all names are spelled correctly and that the exact legal description is given in any documents that will be recorded. Again, errors in such documents and papers will prove time consuming and costly to the parties involved in the transaction.

Making expenditures. The experienced real estate broker will not disburse any of the funds held in trust for a client without considering all important factors. For example, advancing any of the sale proceeds before the transaction is completely closed could lead to serious consequences for the broker if the transaction is not completed as planned. For example, a broker should not order the preparation of a $125 title policy and $40 credit report when only $50 earnest money has been placed in the trust account. The trust accounting for a specific transaction must always balance; disbursements should not exceed the amount of money currently on deposit in that account.

Closing Statements

In every transaction the listing or designated closing broker is responsible for the correctness of the closing statements and for their delivery to the buyer and seller. This is required by the Idaho Real Estate Commission's Rules and Regulations. The broker is not required to prepare the statements personally but is always held responsible for the accuracy of their content.

In the event of a cooperative sale, the earnest money agreement will state which broker is responsible for the closing of the transaction.

Customarily in Idaho separate statements are prepared for the buyer and the seller. The statements, which may be delivered in person or by registered mail, should be signed and a signed copy returned to the broker. The buyer's and seller's signatures on their respective closing statements provide proof of statement delivery. If such statements are sent by certified mail with return receipt requested, a copy of the broker's letter, which accompanies the statement and acknowledges that the statement is enclosed, is sufficient proof of delivery, whether or not the recipient of the statement returns a signed copy to the broker.

In addition the broker must keep a true copy of each closing statement in his or her records for three years after the year in which the transaction was closed, along with copies of all other documents pertinent to the transaction, including the trust account records. This is required so that the Idaho real estate inspector may examine the broker's records of completed transactions as described in Chapter 13 of this Supplement. In addition the broker's copies of the closing statements may provide an invaluable service to a buyer or seller who has lost his or her copy and needs information to complete an income tax return.

In effect the closing statement provides written evidence of the financial history of a transaction. A completed statement should include four parts:

1. a detailed account of the buyer's expenses and credits so that the buyer will know exactly what amounts have been expended in his or her behalf, what amounts have been credited and how much money to bring to the closing,

2. a complete accounting to the seller of expenses and credits and the amount of money to be realized from the sale,

3. a detailed record of cash received by the broker and any disbursements made from that money (this reflects the accounting of the broker's trust fund for the transaction.), and

4. a showing of the amount of commission paid to the broker and an indication of how that fee was divided within the broker's office.

The closing problem at the end of this chapter includes an example of a closing statement form. This particular form is divided into four separate statements—one for the buyer, one for the seller, one for the trust fund accounting of cash received and disbursed and one for the distribution of the broker's commission. Each of these accountings stands as a separate statement and may be understood without consulting the other three.

Closing Action

Before the day of closing the broker must advise both buyer and seller of the exact time and place of the closing. Usually the parties' spouses also must be present. A recent Idaho Supreme Court ruling requires that, whenever such a sales transaction involves the community property of a husband and wife, both spouses must execute (sign) any documents necessary for the transaction, such as the seller's deed to the buyer or the buyer's loan documents.

Many Idaho brokers prefer to close separately with the buyer and seller, holding that each party's financial considerations and arrangements are his or her private business. Generally such brokers meet with the buyer first to accept payment of the sales price and take care of all details involving the buyer; then, after the buyer's check has cleared, they meet with the seller to complete the closing. To close with the buyer first, however, the broker must have the deed and other papers prepared and signed by the seller before the closing. This is so that the buyer can be given copies of the documents at closing. If a new or existing loan is involved, the buyer usually will close at the lending institution. In this case the seller's deed and assignment of the mortgage or trust deed (if there is an assumption) must be signed in advance and given by the broker to the lender before the buyer's closing.

Prior to the closing the broker should inform the buyer of how much cash to bring to the closing. If large amounts are involved, the buyer should bring a cashier's check for the required sum. The broker also must make arrangements for the transfer of the keys to the property so that the buyer can gain access to the premises on the date of possession.

Buyer. At the closing the broker explains the closing statement to the buyer and the buyer, executes documents. All arrangements should be made in advance for the following papers so that they are completely prepared and awaiting the buyer's signature (unless they have been signed in advance):

1. note and mortgage or trust deed, if a new loan is involved,

2. contract of sale and escrow instructions, if the sale is made on contract (installment contract),

3. closing statement, and

4. any other documents in the transaction that require the buyer's signature.

The broker collects from the buyer the amount indicated in the closing statement and delivers the following items to the buyer either at the closing or shortly thereafter:

1. closing statement,

2. copy of note and mortgage or trust deed (if possible), if a new loan is involved or if an existing loan is assumed,

3. copy of contract, signed by the seller, and the escrow instructions (if the sale is made on contract),

4. deed (after it is recorded),

5. copy of insurance policy, whether new or transferred coverage,

6. copy of house plans (if available), and

7. copy of survey (if available).

Seller. When closing with the seller, the broker also must make certain that the seller understands the closing statement, including the broker's accounting of cash received and disbursed in connection with the transaction. Any existing liens not being assumed by the buyer are paid off at this time. If the broker is paying off an existing mortgage or trust deed loan for the seller and the lender is an individual rather than a lending institution, the broker should not disburse the check to the lender until a release of mortgage or deed of reconveyance and the canceled loan documents are received from that lender.

In addition the seller executes the following documents, which may be signed in advance:

1.   closing statement (should indicate the seller's new mailing address),

2.   deed,

3.   contract of sale and escrow instructions (if the sale is made on contract),

4.   assignment of tax and insurance reserve account funds (if existing loan is assumed by buyer),

5.   assignment of fire insurance policy required by lender (if existing loan is assumed by buyer),

6.   discount agreement (if any), and

7.   any other documents in the transaction that require the seller's signature.

The broker pays the seller the amount indicated on the closing statement. If the seller is married the check should be made payable to both spouses. In addition to the sale proceeds the seller receives the following:

1.   closing statement,

2.   old note and mortgage or trust deed (when received from lender), if existing loan is paid off,

3.   release of mortgage or deed of reconveyance (after it is recorded), if existing loan is paid off,

4.   copy of contract and escrow instructions, if sale is being made on contract, and

5.   canceled insurance policy (if any).

Recording. Finally the broker must make sure all documents in the transaction that should be recorded are filed with the county recorder. Such documents include the seller's deed to the buyer, the buyer's new mortgage or trust deed, the seller's release of mortgage or deed of reconveyance, if an old loan was paid off, and any documents necessary to clear the seller's title. These documents should be checked for correctness and completeness before they are recorded. Usually the recordings can be handled through the title insurance company if the broker gives the title company complete instructions on where to deliver the various documents after they have been recorded.

Escrow closings. Frequently, real estate sales transactions will be closed in escrow, as described in Chapters 10 and 23 of the text. Any person may serve as an escrow closing agent in Idaho; such persons are not required to be licensed. However, many persons or entities who serve in this capacity (such as title insurance companies, financial institutions and attorneys) governed and subject to review by some other state or federal agency. An escrow closing does not relieve the broker from responsibility for the correctness and delivery of the closing statement.

Whenever a property is sold on contract, a separate escrow arrangement is usually set up for that contract and the contract remains in escrow until the buyer makes the final payment and obtains title to the property.

CLOSING PROBLEM

Complete the closing statement form found in Figure 23.1. Using the facts given in the following description of a real estate transaction,

Data. On September 9, 1990, Jeff and Ronna Graham accept an offer to purchase their home from Mark and Sarah Swenson. The purchase price is $87,500, and a seven percent commission is to be paid to the real estate brokerage firm of Wilson, Wagner & Bills. The earnest money contract is accompanied with a cashier's check for $1,000 made payable to First Title Insurance Company Escrow.

A first deed of trust recorded against the property has an unpaid principal balance of $63,095.59 as of September 1, 1990. The principal and interest payment on this VA loan, which is to be assumed by the buyers, is $582.48 per month including interest at 10.25 percent per annum, plus tax and insurance reserves of $121.52. The September payment has been made. An assumption fee of one percent on the unpaid principal balance will be charged by the lender. There is a reserve account for taxes and insurance with a balance of $1,096.57. (*Note:* Reserves must be purchased by the buyer; the October payment will be paid through closing and there is no late charge or penalty.)

The Swensons have at least $15,500 plus their share of the closing costs to put toward the purchase price. The Grahams have agreed to carry $8,900 on a second deed of trust payable at $1,500 per year plus interest at 10.5 percent per annum for five years. The first payment will be due the First Title Insurance Company's escrow department one year after the closing date of October 15, 1990.

First Title Insurance Company's escrow closing fees are $2.50 per thousand, or portion thereof, of purchase price plus $30 or $75, whichever is higher. Unless otherwise agreed, buyers and sellers equally split the cost of this service. (No agreements to the contrary have been made.) The title insurance fee charged the seller will be $420, the recording fee for the deed is $2 and for the deed of trust it is $10.

Real estate taxes for 1989 were $960 and were completely paid by June 20, 1990. (*Note:* 1990 taxes are not available; use 1989 taxes.) An existing LID for a sewer district has an outstanding balance of $2,400 plus interest at 9.25 percent per annum. The annual principal and interest payment on the LID has been paid through December 31, 1989. The Swensons have agreed to assume the four remaining equal payments after proration for the current year.

Insurance will be provided by Farmers Insurance Corporation for the buyers. Their first year's premium will be $255.

Personal property, which includes a washer, dryer and window air-conditioner, is to be purchased by the Swensons for a total of $625. This purchase is separate from the real estate transaction but is included in the closing statement.

The Swensons were referred by the Trans-national Relocation Company and are entitled to a 20 percent referral fee based on the commission generated to the selling broker.

(*Note:* Compute all prorations on the basis of a 360-day year/30-day month. Carry computations to three decimal places and round off when the computation is complete. Check your solution with the one given in the Answer Key for this Supplement.)

Figure 23.1   Closing Statement Form

CLOSING STATEMENT

Sale No. _____

Seller _____

Buyer _____

Property _____

Salesman _____ Pro Rate Date _____

	BUYER		SELLER	
	DEBIT	CREDIT	DEBIT	CREDIT
Purchase Price				
Earnest money paid				
Subsequent payment				
Assumption/Loan Payoff				
First Mortgage Balance				
Interest				
Reserves				
Taxes				
Insurance				
FHA Insurance				
Assumption Fee				
Discount Points				
Contract Balance				
Interest				
New Mortgage Taken Out By Buyer				
Reserve for Taxes, Ins, Etc.				
Credit Report				
Loan Service Fee				
Appraisal Fee				
Interest Adj.				
MGIC Prem.				
Contract Or Note Given Seller				
Taxes				
Special Assessments				
Fire Insurance				
Rent				
Title Insurance & Ata				
Recording & Releases				
Attorneys' Fees				
Escrow Fee				
Broker's Commission				
Cash From Buyer To Close				
Amount Paid To Seller				
Balance				

Prepared by _____

Date _____

_____

_____

A P P R O V E D

Buyer _____

Buyer _____

Seller _____

Seller _____

Answer Key

Check your answers. If you did not answer a question correctly, *restudy the course material until you understand the correct answer.*

Chapter 4
1. c
2. a
3. d
4. c
5. c
6. b

Chapter 5
1. b
2. b
3. a
4. c
5. d

Chapter 6
1. b
2. d
3. d
4. a
5. b
6. b
7. d
8. a

Chapter 7
1. d
2. c
3. c

Chapter 8
1. d
2. a
3. b
4. d
5. a
6. d

Chapter 9
1. a
2. b
3. d
4. c
5. a
6. c
7. d
8. c
9. a
10. d
11. d

Chapter 10
For answer to earnest money problem, *see* pages 44–45

1. c
2. d
3. c
4. b
5. a
6. b
7. a
8. d
9. c
10. b

Chapter 11
1. c
2. b
3. a
4. d
5. c
6. c
7. a
8. a

Chapter 12
1. b
2. c
3. b
4. d
5. d
6. c

Chapter 13
1. b
2. c
3. c
4. a
5. b
6. d
7. b
8. c
9. b
10. d
11. b
12. c
13. a
14. c
15. c
16. a
17. d
18. c

Chapter 14 / 15
1. c
2. a
3. c
4. a
5. d
6. d
7. a
8. b
9. d

Chapter 14/ 15 (Continued)
10. d
11. a

Chapter 16
1. c
2. b
3. d
4. c
5. b
6. b
7. d
8. a
9. d
10. b

Chapter 18
1. d
2. d
3. d

Chapter 19
1. b
2. c
3. a
4. c
5. b
6. d
7. b
8. c

Chapter 21
1. c
2. d
3. a
4. c

Chapter 23

The completed closing statement is shown on page 121.

Closing statement computations:

The problem states that the payments are current to September 1 and because interest is paid in arrears, we must charge the seller interest to the date of closing.

> September 1 to October 15 = 45 days interest owed
> $63,095.59 × 10.25% = $6,467.2979 per year
> $6,467.2979 ÷ 12 = $538.9415 per month
> $538.9415 ÷ 30 = $17.9647 per day
> $17,9647 × 45 days = $808.41

The reserve account is a savings account for the seller to pay the taxes and insurance when due. Because we are charging the seller for the taxes, we must have the buyer buy the reserves to pay the taxes and insurance premiums as needed.

The real estate tax bills are not mailed out until the first week in November; therefore we do not know the exact amount of taxes owed for the current year. We will prorate taxes based on the most recent information available; thus we use 1989 taxes as a figure. Idaho's tax year is from January 1 to December 31.

> January 1 to October 15 = 9 months and 15 days
> $960 ÷ 12 = $80
> $80 × 9.5 months = $760

Because the taxes cannot be paid the buyer is assuming the liability for the full payment when due, so we give the buyer credit for the seller's share of the taxes owed and charge the seller accordingly.

The LID is handled the same way the taxes were handled, except an interest payment also is due.

> January 1 to October 15 = 9 months and 15 days
> $2,400 ÷ 4 = $600
> $600 ÷ 12 = $50
> $50 × 9.5 months = $475
> plus
> $2,400 × 9.25% = $222
> $222 ÷ 12 = $18.5
> $18 × 9.5 = $175.75

The escrow closing fee is to be shared equally by the buyer and seller. The fee is computed at $2.50 per thousand dollar value or portion thereof. Because $87,500 is more than $87,000, the fee is computed as though the price was $88,000.

> $2.50 × 88 = $220 + $30 = $250
> 1/2 × $250 = $125

Completed Closing Statement

CLOSING STATEMENT

Sale No. _1990-241_

Seller ___GRAHAM, JEFF AND RONNA___

Buyer ___SWENSON, MARK AND SARAH___

Property ___1313 HONEY LOCUST DRIVE, BOISE, IDAHO___

Salesman ___FRANK LIVERMORE___   Pro Rate Date ___OCTOBER 15, 1990___

	BUYER		SELLER	
	DEBIT	CREDIT	DEBIT	CREDIT
Purchase Price	87,500.00			87,500.00
Earnest money paid _September 9, 1990_	1,000.00			
Subsequent payment				
Assumption/LOAN PAYOFF				
First Mortgage Balance _as of 9/1/90_		63,095.59	63,095.59	
Interest _from 9/1/90 to 10/15/90_		808.41	808.41	
Reserves	1,096.57			1,096.57
Taxes				
Insurance				
FHA Insurance				
Assumption Fee _1% of unpaid balance_	630.96			
Discount Points				
October payment to lender	704.00			
Contract Balance				
Interest				
New Mortgage Taken Out By Buyer				
Reserve for Taxes, Ins, Etc.				
Credit Report				
Loan Service Fee				
Appraisal Fee				
Interest Adj.				
MGIC Prem.				
Contract Or Note Given Seller _2nd Trust Deed_		8,900.00	8,900.00	
Taxes _1990 Estimate (buyer assumed)_		760.00	760.00	
Special Assessments _L.I.D. plus interest_ (buyer assumed)		650.75	650.75	
Fire Insurance _First year premium_	255.00			
Rent				
Title Insurance & Ats _Owners Policy_			420.00	
Recording & Releases _Warranty Deed and_ 2nd Deed of Trust	12.00			
Personal property: washer, dryer and air conditioner	625.00			625.00
Attorneys' Fees				
Escrow Fee _shared equally_	125.00		125.00	
Broker's Commission			6,125.00	
Cash From Buyer To Close		15,733.78		
Amount Paid To Seller			8,336.82	
Balance	90,948.53	90,948.53	89,221.57	89,221.57

Prepared by _First Title Insurance Escrow_

Date _October 15, 1990_

A
P
P
R
O
V
E
D

Buyer _____

Buyer _____

Seller _____

Seller _____

Completed Real Estate Purchase and Sale Agreement and Receipt for Earnest Money

REAL ESTATE PURCHASE AND SALE AGREEMENT AND RECEIPT FOR EARNEST MONEY
(This form to be used ONLY by members of the National Association of REALTORS)

This contract stipulates the terms of sale of the property. Read carefully before signing (including information on reverse side). This is a legally binding contract. IF YOU HAVE ANY QUESTIONS, CONSULT YOUR ATTORNEY BEFORE SIGNING.

_____ Boise _____, Idaho September 9, 19 90

MARK SWENSON AND SARAH SWENSON, Husband and Wife
(hereinafter called "Buyer") agrees to purchase, and the undersigned Seller agrees to sell the following described real estate hereinafter referred to as "premises"
commonly known as __1313 HONEY LOCUST DRIVE__
City of __BOISE__ County of __ADA__, Idaho legally described as: __Lot 13 Block 3 of The Randolf Addition to Boise, book 10 page 12 of plats, Ada County, Idaho__
(A FULL AND COMPLETE LEGAL DESCRIPTION MUST BE INSERTED, ATTACHED OR WRITTEN ON THE REVERSE HEREOF PRIOR TO EXECUTION BY SELLER. Buyer hereby authorizes broker to insert over his signature the correct legal description of the premises if unavailable at the time of signing, or to correct the legal description previously entered if erroneous or incomplete.)

EARNEST MONEY.
(a) Buyer hereby deposits as earnest money and a receipt is hereby acknowledged of __ONE THOUSAND AND no/100-------------__ dollars
(s __1,000.00__) evidenced by: ☐Cash ☐Personal Check ☒Cashiers Check ☐Note Due ☐or _____
(b) Earnest Money to be deposited in trust account upon acceptance by all parties and shall be held by ☐Listing Broker ☐Selling Broker ☐Other __First Title Insurance Co.__ for the benefit of the parties hereto, and __Gold Carpet Realty, Sam Livermore__ (Broker) shall hold the completely executed broker's copy of this agreement and is responsible for the closing.
(c) If all conditions have been met by Buyer, Buyer and Seller agree that the earnest money (less credit report fees, and any other Buyer's costs) shall be refunded to Buyer in the event the financing contemplated herein by Buyer is not obtainable.
(d) The parties agree that __First Title Insurance__ Title Company shall provide said title policy and preliminary report of commitment and the "closing agent" for this transaction shall be __First Title Insurance Co.__ If a long-term escrow/collection is involved, then the escrow holder shall be __First Title Insurance Co.__

1. **TOTAL PURCHASE PRICE IS** __EIGHTY-SEVEN THOUSAND FIVE HUNDRED AND NO/100__ DOLLARS ($ __87,500.00__)
payable as follows:
a. $ __15,500.00__ Cash down, including above Earnest Money (Closing costs are additional).
b. $ __72,000.00__ Balance of the purchase price (M.I.P. not included).

2. **FINANCING.** This agreement is contingent upon Buyer qualifying for:
☐FHA ☐VA ☐Conventional ☐IHA. Purchase loan balance as noted above for a period of __N/A__ years at __N/A__ % per annum. (If FHA or VA loan is sought, read the applicable provisions on the reverse side hereof.) Buyer shall pay no more than __N/A__ points plus origination fee if any. Seller to pay only the discount points necessary in order to obtain above described financing but not to exceed __N/A__ %.
☒Buyer to ASSUME and ☐ will ☐ will not be required to qualify for an EXISTING LOAN(S) of approximately $ __63,100.00__ at no more than 10¼ % with monthly payments of approximately $ __704.00__ P ☒☐☐☐ ☐☒ This agreement ☐is ☒is not contingent upon Lender releasing Seller's liability.
Type of loan __VA__. Buyer shall apply for such loan or assumption within three (3) banking days after Seller's acceptance of this agreement.
OTHER FINANCING, TERMS & CONDITIONS: __Seller agrees to carry a 2nd Deed of Trust in the amount of $ 8,900.00 payable in annual installments of $ 1,500.00 plus interest at 10½ % per annum. The first payment is due October 15, 1991. Any remaining unpaid balance will be all due and payable in five (5) years from date of closing.__

3. **THIS AGREEMENT** ☐Is ☒is not **CONTINGENT** upon sale and closing of __N/A__ on or before __N/A__ listed with __N/A__
(If a contingency is noted please read applicable conditions in Paragraph # 15 on reverse side. NOTE: Any waiver by the Buyer under this section will be a waiver of ALL contingencies, including financing.)

4. **ITEMS SPECIFICALLY INCLUDED** IN THIS SALE (if FHA/VA financing is sought see Item # 14 on reverse side): __New G.E. washer and dryer plus a one year old R.C.A. Whirlpool air conditioner (serial numbers to be provided by seller)__

5. **ITEMS SPECIFICALLY EXCLUDED** IN THIS SALE: __N/A__

6. **COSTS PAID BY:** Costs in addition to those listed below may be incurred by Buyer and Seller. Unless otherwise agreed herein, or provided by law or required by lender, Buyer shall purchase Seller's reserve account if loan assumption.
☐Yes ☒No. Purchaser's Extended Coverage Title Policy requested. Additional premium paid by __N/A__. See item # 17 on reverse side.
If requested by lender or otherwise stated herein, the below costs will be paid as indicated.

Costs Paid By	Appraisal	Loan Assumpt.	Well Inspect.	Pump/Inspect Septic	City/County Code Inspect. if required	Contract and/or Document Prep.	Closing Agent's Fee	Long Term Escrow Fees	Lender or Code Repairs	
BUYER		X								
N/A	X		X	X					X	
SELLER										
SHARE EQUALLY				X	X	X	X			

Cost of lender or code repairs not to exceed $ __N/A__ Discount points to be paid as agreed on line 29 and 30. SELLER UNDERSTANDS that as a result of any city or county inspections HE MAY BE REQUIRED TO MAKE REPAIRS to the property in order to comply with the housing code WHETHER OR NOT A SALE IS COMPLETED UNDER THIS AGREEMENT.

7. **POSSESSION.** Buyer shall be entitled to possession on ☒ closing ☐ other __N/A__. "Closing" means the date on which all documents are either recorded or accepted by an escrow agent and the sale proceeds are available to Seller. Taxes and water assessments (using the last available assessment as a basis), rents, insurance premiums, interest and reserves on liens, encumbrances or obligations assumed shall be pro-rated as of __October 15, 1990__. Buyer shall pay for fuel in tank, amount to be determined by the supplier at Seller's expense.

8. **CLOSING.** On or before the closing date, Buyer and Seller shall deposit with the closing agent all funds and instruments necessary to complete the sale. The closing date shall be no later than __October 15, 1990__.

9. **ACCEPTANCE.** Buyer's offer is made subject to the acceptance of Seller on or before 12:00 o'clock midnight of __September 9, 1990__. If Seller does not accept this agreement within the time specified, the entire Earnest Money shall be refunded to Buyer on demand. Seller's counter offer (if any) is made subject to the acceptance of Buyer on or before 12:00 o'clock midnight of __September 9, 1990__. TIME IS OF THE ESSENCE OF THIS AGREEMENT.

10. **IMPORTANT - AGENCY DISCLOSURE:** At the time of signing this agreement the agent working with the buyer represented __the SELLER__ and the agent working with the seller represented __the SELLER__. Each party signing this document confirms that prior written disclosure of agency was provided to him/her in this transaction. Each party to this transaction has read and understands the contents of the agency disclosure brochure previously received.

Listing Agency: __Wilson, Wagner & Bills__ Selling Agency: __Gold Carpet Realty__
By: __N/A__ Phone: _____ By: __Frank Livermore__ Phone: _____
Buyer: __(signature) Mark Swenson__ Buyer's Address: _____
Buyer: __(signature) Sarah Swenson__ Buyer's Phone: Residence _____ Business _____

On this date, I/We hereby approve and accept the sale set forth in the above agreement and agree to carry out all the terms thereof on the part of the Seller and the undersigned further agrees to pay a total brokerage fee of __$ 6,125.00 or seven percent__ to the above named Broker(s) for services. Brokerage fee will be paid in cash unless otherwise agreed in writing.
I/We further acknowledge receipt of a true copy of this agreement signed by both parties.
Seller: __(signature) Jeff Graham__ Date: __9/9/90__ Seller's Address: __1313 Honey Locust Drive__
Seller: __(signature) Ronna Graham__ Date: __9/9/90__ Seller's Phone: Residence _____ Business _____

A true copy of the foregoing agreement, signed by the Seller and containing the full and complete legal description of the premises, is hereby received on this __9th__ day of __September__, 19 __90__
Buyer: __(signature)__ Buyer: __(signature)__
THE PROVISIONS CONTAINED ON THE REVERSE SIDE OF THIS PAGE SHALL ALSO CONSTITUTE PART OF THE AGREEMENT OF THE PARTIES. EACH OF THE PARTIES ACKNOWLEDGES READING THIS AGREEMENT IN FULL.
Buyer's initial _____ Seller's initial _____   **BROKER'S COPY**   RE 21 REV. 2/90

Completed Real Estate Purchase and Sale Agreement and Receipt for Earnest Money (Continued)

11. **DEFAULT AND ATTORNEY'S FEES.** If Seller executes this agreement, and title to said premises is marketable and insurable and the Buyer neglects or refuses to comply with the terms or any conditions of sale within five (5) days from the date on which said term or condition is to be complied with, then the Earnest Money shall be forfeited and considered as liquidated damages to Seller, and Buyer's interest in the premises shall be immediately terminated. The broker shall pay from said Earnest Money the costs of title insurance, escrow fees, attorney fees and any other expenses directly incurred in connection with this transaction and the remainder shall be apportioned one-half to the Seller and one-half to the broker, provided the amount to broker does not exceed the agreed commission. Such forfeiture and acceptance by Seller and broker of the Earnest Money as liquidated damages does not constitute a waiver of other remedies available to Seller and broker.

In the event of default by either of the parties in their performance of the terms and conditions of this agreement, the defaulting party agrees to pay all attorney fees and costs incurred by the non-defaulting party.

In the event of a dispute between the parties as to the Earnest Money deposited hereunder by Buyer, the Broker, holding the Earnest Money deposit may file an interpleader action in a court of competent jurisdiction to resolve any such dispute between the parties. The Buyer and the Seller authorize the Broker holding the Earnest Money deposit to utilize as much of the Earnest Money deposit as may be necessary to advance the costs and fees required for filing of any such action.

12. **INCLUDED ITEMS.** All attached floor coverings, attached television antenna, attached plumbing, bathroom and lighting fixtures, window screens, screen doors, storm windows, storm doors, window coverings, exterior trees, plants, or shrubbery, water heating apparatus and fixtures, attached fireplace equipment, awnings, ventilating, cooling and heating systems, built in and "drop in" ranges (but excepting all other ranges), fuel tanks and irrigation fixtures and equipment, and any and all, if any, water and water rights, and any and all, if any, ditches and ditch rights that are appurtenant thereto that are now on or used in connection with the premises shall be included in the sale unless otherwise provided herein.

13. **FINANCING REQUIREMENTS.** If financing is required, the Buyer agrees to make a best effort to procure same and further agrees to make application therefore within three (3) banking days after Seller's acceptance of this agreement. If VA or FHA financing is contemplated, additional provisions pertaining thereto may be attached thereto and are thereby incorporated herein by reference.

14. **FHA/VA.** If this agreement is contingent upon Buyer obtaining FHA or VA financing, Buyer and Seller agree that, notwithstanding any other provisions of this contract, Buyer shall not be obligated to complete the purchase of the property described herein **unless** Buyer has received a written statement issued by the FHA or VA as applicable setting forth an appraised value of the property (excluding closing costs) equal to or greater than the purchase price herein. The Buyer may, nevertheless, at his sole discretion proceed under the terms of this agreement provided he shall agree to pay in cash the difference between the asking price stated herein and the appraised value. Buyer shall in either circumstance be obligated to pay normal closing costs attributable to Buyer including but not limited to credit report fees and other loan charges. **The appraised valuation is arrived at to determine the maximum mortgage the Department of Housing and Urban Development will insure. HUD does not warrant the value or the condition of the property. The purchaser should satisfy himself/herself that the price and the condition of the property are acceptable.**

It is agreed that any item included in Paragraph #4 is of nominal value less than $100.

Seller understands that in order for a Buyer to finance through FHA, VA or a conventional lender, those agencies may require that the property comply with the housing code and other governmental requirements of the city or county in which it is located, and may require other inspections. Seller authorizes the selling agent herein to request a City Code Compliance inspection. Seller agrees to pay, in advance, upon request of agent, costs of any of the above inspections.

15. **CONTINGENCY CLAUSE.** If Buyer's offer is contingent upon certain specified conditions occurring, as specified in Item #3 of this agreement, Seller shall have the right to continue to offer the herein property for sale and to accept offers until such time as said contingencies have been satisfied or waived by Buyer. Should Seller receive another acceptable offer to purchase, Seller shall give Buyer three banking days written notice of such offer. In the event Buyer does not waive or satisfy the contingencies within the three-day period, then this Agreement shall be terminated and all deposits returned to Buyer less customary Buyer's costs. In the event Buyer does waive or satisfy the contingencies then Buyer shall proceed to purchase the property under the remaining terms and conditions of this Agreement notwithstanding that the terms of the new offer may be more or less favorable. Notice shall be considered given and the three days shall commence on the earlier of either personal delivery of notice to the Buyer or his agent or two days following the date of mailing evidenced by the postmark on the envelope containing such notice. Notice shall expire at midnight on the third banking day after notice. All notices shall be sent to the addresses shown on the front page of this agreement.

NOTE: Any waiver by the Buyer under this section will be a waiver of ALL contingencies, including financing.

16. **TITLE INSURANCE.** The Seller shall within a reasonable time after closing furnish to the Buyer a title insurance policy in the amount of the purchase price of the premises showing marketable and insurable title subject to the liens, encumbrances and defects elsewhere set out in this agreement to be discharged or assumed by the Buyer. Prior to closing the transaction, the Seller shall furnish to the Buyer a commitment for a title insurance policy showing the condition of the title to said premises. Buyer shall have five (5) days from receipt of the commitment or until 24 hours prior to closing, whichever is the less, within which to object in writing to the condition of the title as set forth in the report. If the Buyer does not so object, the Buyer shall be deemed to have accepted the conditions of the title. It is agreed that if the title of said premises is not marketable, or cannot be made so within thirty (30) days after notice containing a written statement of defects is delivered to the Seller, or if the Seller, having approved said sale fails to consummate the same as herein agreed, the earnest money shall be returned to the Buyer and Seller shall pay for the cost of title insurance, escrow and legal fees, if any.

17. **EXTENDED COVERAGE TITLE POLICY.** A standard policy of title insurance does not cover certain potential problems or risks such as liens (i.e., a legal claim against property for payment of some debt or obligation), boundary disputes, claims of easement, and other matters or claims if they are not of **public record** at time of closing. However, under Idaho law, such potential claims against the property may have become legal obligation **before** the purchase of the home and yet may **not** be of public record until after the purchase. For example, Idaho law allows workmen who have built a new home or repaired or remodeled an existing one to file liens against that property for a period of time after they last worked on the home. The debt in such cases will become a lien or claim against the property itself and, if not paid by the Seller, must be paid by the Buyer to protect the equity in the home. Title insurance companies may be able to issue an "extended coverage" policy for an additional premium. In addition to the premium for extended coverage title policy, there may be other costs involved (i.e., survey, additional closing fees). Such a policy **may** protect the Buyer against problems such as the above. Of course, even an "extended coverage" policy contains exclusions and will not insure against all potential problems or risks involved in buying property. It is recommended that the Buyer talk to a title insurance company about what it offers in the way of extended coverage. Only the policy itself can tell exactly what type of coverage is offered, so contact a title insurance company for particulars.

18. **TITLE CONVEYANCE.** Title of Seller is to be conveyed by warranty deed, unless otherwise provided, and is to be marketable and insurable except for rights reserved in federal patents, state or railroad deeds, building or use restrictions, building and zoning regulations and ordinances of any governmental unit, and rights of way and easements established or of record. Liens, encumbrances or defects to be discharged by Seller may be paid out of purchase money at date of closing. No liens, encumbrances or defects, which are to be discharged or assumed by Buyer or to which title is taken subject to, exists unless otherwise specified herein on the front page of this agreement under OTHER FINANCING, TERMS & CONDITIONS.

19. **RISK OF LOSS.** Prior to closing of this sale, all risk of loss shall remain with the Seller. In addition, should the premises be materially damaged by fire or other cause prior to closing, this agreement shall be voidable at the option of the Buyer.

20. **INSPECTION.** The Buyer hereby acknowledges further that he has not received or relied upon any statements or representation by the broker or his representatives or by the Seller which are not herein expressed. The Buyer has entered into this agreement relying solely upon information and knowledge obtained from his own investigation or personal inspection of the premises. This agreement constitutes the whole agreement between the parties and no warranties, including any warranty of habitability, agreements or representations have been made or shall be binding upon either party unless herein set forth.

Each of the parties acknowledges reading and understanding this agreement in full.

Buyer's initial MS & SS   Seller's initial JG & RG

STATE OF IDAHO   )
                                                        : ss
County of   ADA   )
On this ____9th____ day of __September__, 19 _90_, before me, the undersigned, a Notary Public in and for said state, personally appeared Jeff Graham and Ronna Graham   ,
known to me to be the person(s) who signed the foregoing instrument as Seller and acknowledged to me that ____t he y____ executed the same. IN WITNESS WHEREOF, I have hereunto set my hand and affixed my seal the day and year first above written.

Notary Public for Idaho ____(Notary signature and seal)__ Residing at ____Boise_____

Index

YOUR SATISFACTION IS GUARANTEED!

All books come with a 30 day money-back guarantee. If you are not completely satisfied, simply return your books and your money will be refunded in full.

☐ Please send me the Real Estate Education Company catalog featuring your full list of titles.

Prices are subject to change without notice.
Also available in your local bookstore.

Fill out form and mail today!

Or Save $1.00 when you order by Fax: 312-836-1021.

Name_____

Address _____

City/State/Zip _____

Telephone (_____) _____

Payment must accompany all orders (check one):
☐ Check or money order (payable to Dearborn Financial Publishing, Inc., 520 North Dearborn Street, Chicago, Illinois 60610-4354)
☐ Charge to my credit card:
   ☐ VISA   ☐ MasterCard

Account No. _____ Exp. Date _____

Signature _____
(All charge orders must be signed.)

Return Address:

_____

_____

BUSINESS REPLY MAIL
FIRST CLASS   PERMIT NO. 88176   CHICAGO, IL

POSTAGE WILL BE PAID BY ADDRESSEE:

**Real Estate
Education Company**
Order Department
520 North Dearborn Street
Chicago, Illinois 60610-9857

NO POSTAGE
NECESSARY
IF MAILED
IN THE
UNITED STATES

IMPORTANT · PLEASE FOLD OVER · PLEASE TAPE BEFORE MAILING

NOTE: This page, when folded over and taped, becomes a postage-free envelope, which has been approved by the United States Postal Service. It is provided for your convenience.

IMPORTANT · PLEASE FOLD OVER · PLEASE TAPE BEFORE MAILING